DEX

CANES
IN THE
DUNGEON

PAIN AND
PLEASURE

Printed in the United States of America

Library of Congress Cataloging-in-Publication Data

Dex, 1955-

Canes in the Dungeon: Pain and Pleasure by Dex

ISBN-13: 979-8-9922239-4-1 (paperback)

       979-8-9922239-5-8 (Ebook-Kindle)

       979-8-9922239-6-5 (Ebook-Epub)

Sex and sexuality, 2. BDSM, 3. Energy exchange, 4. Caning,

5. Leather lifestyle, 6. Dungeon play, 7. Bastinado

First Edition,

Joan's Books

Tampa, FL

Table of Contents

Preface

I BOUGHT MY first canes from Hanson Paddle at the Boston Fetish Flea Market in 2001. They were three raw, unfinished rattan canes. Although I didn't know it at the time, it was beneficial that they were raw rattan, as it provided me with a safe, lightweight stick suitable for a beginner cane top. I knew right away that it would be one of my favorite types of dungeon play, and I wanted to learn more about it.

I was fortunate, early in my caning journey, to be befriended by an experienced cane top while attending a munch in Hampton, VA. Lady Hugs was happy to share what she knew about caning. She had even written a short article titled "The Art of Caning." I absorbed all the information I could and applied it in practice. I continued to learn about caning by attending classes at BDSM conventions, watching other enthusiasts in action, and practicing on different cane bottoms (no pun intended).

One might think there is not much to learn about caning. After all, you pick up a stick and hit someone's butt, right? Well, yes, that is true, but there are definitely ways to up your game from that starting point. I've been teaching caning workshops for twenty years.

I decided that the techniques that sprang from Lady Hug's essay and were greatly expanded upon over the years deserve to be preserved in a book. So, here we are.

I highly recommend reading the book in conjunction with watching the instructional videos on The Leather Journey YouTube channel and also at *http://witd.houseofgraves.com*. The Whips in the Dungeon website, hosted and sponsored by Master Graves, is ad-free, subscription-free, and has all of my videos unedited. This repository of companion videos is a valuable addition to anyone reading the book and wanting to become skilled with a cane.

Acknowledgments

WHYPPIE (WHYPDANCER) AT Canes4Pain is perhaps the most famous and sought-after cane maker in the U.S. BDSM scene. I am fortunate to own an extensive collection of her crown-jewel canes – each a unique and beautiful work of art. Not only are they visually appealing, but, more importantly, they have great energy, balance, and excellent tonals.

Before she made me this marvelous set of canes, I was using what in her terms would be called sticks. They were raw rattan canes that had never been seasoned.

Not only did Whyppie make me a fabulous set of canes, but she also made me one of every type and style she makes. One could say it represents a complete set or, metaphorically, a full orchestra. Before Whyppie's canes, affectionately known as the Girls, were made, I dabbled in canes, but the Girls inspired me to go deeper.

Hanson Paddle, although it is no longer in business, must be acknowledged. Hanson sold me shorties[1] for years at nearly cost, as they knew I was using them for educational purposes. The shorties served me well in my workshops. Since I have never considered myself an expert in caning, I took the caning enthusiast approach in my workshops. My workshops turned into rock concerts, with attendees — gifted shorties at the door — becoming active participants alongside me as I demonstrated a variety of techniques.

It was after one of these workshops at Thunder in the Mountains

---

1 Shorty. A cane enthusiast's colloquial term to describe a short cane usually 16-20" long that can be used for percussion, OTK (over-the-knee), caning in tight quarters. Anywhere a short stick will work that a longer one would not.

that I was gifted a different sort of cane, or what I would call a pervertible. It began its life as a fly-fishing rod. It was a fiberglass rod that looked like an orchestra conductor's baton. I am grateful to the kind person who gave me that gift, though I can no longer remember their name.

This was also the Thunder in the Mountains where I met Gloryus. She is a significant reason this book is being written. The first time I played with her was transformative for both of us. I had just met her and knew right away that I wanted to share energy with her in a caning scene. She had previously been caned but did not like it. She was hesitant to try it again. Over the course of two days, I discussed my caning style and philosophy with her. I was confident that I could change her opinion on caning.

Gloryus was finally persuaded to bottom for my canes. The connection we developed through caning, along with the energy exchanged in that scene, inspired me to learn more about caning and share that knowledge through teaching.

Master Jim was a quiet and unassuming Dom who taught me a lot about caning. I watched him cane with skill, using what I now call partial strokes, on his lady, Kandace, on many occasions at House Mermaid. He was one of the most skilled caning tops I've ever watched. He never taught a caning class, but led by example in the sacred space. His dungeon play was mesmerizing and such a pleasure to watch.

Cane bottoms through the years have to be mentioned not only for providing fun in the dungeon, but also for frequently serving as my workshop demo bottoms (Moodstone, Trophy_Wife, Nikita, IrishRedHot66). I must also thank Miss Chris, Gloryus, Mr_Arrow, MyWay917, and WhypDancer for providing valuable feedback on the Advanced Reader Edition.

If a picture is worth a thousand words, then this little book is a treasure trove because of the amazing photographers who have contributed their skill, talent, and generous time. This is the third cover photo Tigrrrr and the lovely budddd have done for my books. They have not only provided continuity for the covers but also beautiful cover art photography for the artists at Damonza to work with. The photos inside the book were taken by Zark during a live dungeon play party at Sidetrax, under less than optimal lighting conditions in a setting that was appropriately lit for dungeon play. Ian_Michaels, while vending and teaching workshops at Jax FetFest, took time away to photograph the caning workshop session and capture in stills most of the techniques illustrated in this book. A big thank you to the cane bottoms who appear in this book. Artistic cane marks and ladders were captured by the photography of ATPStudios. Without HelpSophia, IrishRedHot66, KinkySkylarRose, lil_belle and Trophy Wife, this book would be so boring. School discipline photos were taken by WilliamAZ of Miss Chris and Jenni Mack. Whypdancer and Gloryus also contributed photos that add their own special spice to this book.[2]

No book could be complete without someone providing the attention to detail to edit it, and Moodstone is my editor-in-chief. She has been my love, my passion, and my life for the past two decades.

---

2 One of the most challenging aspects of writing a book on canes is illustrating it. One can try to describe three-dimensional space and a cane moving through it to create a particular technique, but a picture is worth a thousand words. A photo captures a moment in time but cannot illustrate movement through three-dimensional space. Therefore, an attempt has been made through the use of an image with an overlay of an arrow in hopes of showing the direction of movement and flow of the cane into the stroke captured by the camera. A fallback is to watch my caning and bastinado instructional videos.

The cane can strike fear into the heart of many bottoms. It is an implement capable of delivering intense sensation to the body with very little effort. As with any tool that carries this level of potential, it also offers flexibility, providing sensations that range from very light kisses and gentle brush strokes to distinct, incremental increases in intensity, all the way up to extreme energy.

This book will provide instruction on a variety of techniques for intentionally delivering different caning energies. It will also cover various rattan diameters and lengths, the array of rods available, the transformation of vanilla implements into canes and rods for play, and different caning styles and rhythms.

The cane has a storied past, most notably with its use as a tool of corporal punishment. In prison settings, it was used to discipline and punish prisoners. In educational settings, particularly in the British school system, the cane was routinely used to discipline unruly children. In some parts of the world, caning is still used in both judicial and school settings.

Parents with unruly children would often, in times past, use a cane to save wear and tear on their hands and maximize the pain. "Spare the rod and spoil the child" was taken quite literally by some parents, though caning, in my opinion, should only be used in consensual play.

Consent is an essential aspect of any dungeon play. Everyone in leather or BDSM should be a consenting adult. Explicit consent must be obtained before any caning scene can take place. A word of caution - in many jurisdictions, caning is considered to be assault, and the law in some jurisdictions does not provide allowance for consent. Caning in dungeon play should be reserved for safe spaces in communities that recognize that consenting play between adults is all in fun among like-minded, intelligent individuals.

Chapter 1

Canes vs Rods

IN DUNGEON VERNACULAR, any stick used to strike a butt might be called a cane. Canes and rods can be made out of a wide variety of materials, and all provide different sensations. The distinction that various cane makers and enthusiasts have taught me is that a rod is made out of an artificial material, and a cane is made out of a natural material.[3]

There are many types of natural material canes. Rattan, bamboo, hardwoods (such as maple, hickory, cherry, and oak), and leather are the most commonly used materials. Birch, or any bush that has long, thin, straight limbs, can also be made into a switch or a bundle for caning/switching.

A. Canes.

Rattan Canes. The traditional cane is made from rattan vine and must be straightened. Rattan has about 600 species of climbing palms across 13 genera, and comes in various forms derived from

---

3 There are even cane-like implements that definitely are not canes, such as a crop, but the shaft of a crop looks like a cane and can be used to cane someone. Actually, only the flap at the end of a crop (the keeper) should be used to strike someone, but the dungeon monitors probably won't stop a scene to tell the top that striking with the shaft is wrong.

the rattan vine's core and outer layers (bark or skin). (Note rattan canes diameters are normally referred to in the metric system of measurement. Hardwood canes are often measured in inches, using the British Imperial system). Rattan breaks cleanly, with little chance of splintering.

Rattan is porous and cannot be 100% sanitized if it comes into contact with blood or bodily fluids. It can, however, be sealed; one common method is to coat it with marine varnish. Marine varnish is specifically designed for exteriors with added UV blockers and flexibility to handle sun/moisture, making it ideal for boats, outdoor furniture and sealed canes. Polyurethane, varnish and shellac will become brittle over time and can become embedded during play. Clear shards are hard to remove from the bottom's skin. Some canes are sealed with natural wax, but wax alas cannot be cleaned and while it seals and adds weight to the cane is no more sanitary than raw rattan. I own raw rattan canes, seasoned rattan canes (conditioned with raw linseed oil), and sealed rattan canes (sealed with a marine varnish). They all serve different purposes in a caning scene.

Raw rattan is lightweight and delivers a light punch unless swung vigorously. It is inexpensive and perfect for the beginning caner to practice with and learn the art of caning. As it ages, unless it has been seasoned, it will dry out and be more prone to breaking than seasoned rattan.

Seasoned or conditioned rattan is denser and capable of providing heavier strikes. Seasoned rattan has been soaked in raw linseed oil for at least 24 hours to condition the cane. Linseed oil will wick into the porous cane, making the cane denser, slightly heavier in the hand, and less likely to break. The cane's exterior can then be sealed with a heavy varnish, such as marine varnish. The cane should always be seasoned before sealing it.

Rattan can be stained different colors prior to finishing. Calamity Canes was one of the first cane makers to create a colorful Painbow. Not all canes are sealed, but the advantage of sealing a cane is that it can be cleaned more easily. In my opinion, the tip of the cane should not be sealed. That way, it can be given a "drink" of raw linseed oil to recondition it a couple of times a year.[4]

Bamboo Canes. Bamboo possesses qualities that may be desirable in a cane. Bamboo wood is easily sourced since it grows quickly. In fact, some varieties of bamboo are considered an invasive species. Bamboo tends to grow straight, so it is easier to make it into a cane than using rattan. Many caning enthusiasts have bamboo in their cane cases.

The major disadvantage of using bamboo as a cane is that it splinters when it breaks. For that reason, I do not recommend using a bamboo cane. Most reputable caning sources will advise against using it.

If one wants to use a bamboo cane, it is better to use a thicker piece of bamboo to avoid splintering. Thick bamboo is strong and is routinely used by rope people for rigging and suspension work. Thick bamboo can be made into bass canes and baritone canes with little chance of breaking.[5]

For the purists, rattan can also be sourced in thick dimensions. The bass cane in my crown jewel set of mermaid canes is rattan. It has phenomenal tonals and provides deep energy that carries and travels through to the bottom.

Leather canes. Leather provides a different caning sensation than rattan and other materials. Different is good—it is all good!

Leather canes can be made several ways. One method is to raw hide is cut into strips, then wet, before being rolled into a stick-shaped cane or twisted into a candy cane shape and dried. A second method sews layers of leather together. They can then be made different thicknesses, widths and lengths. AZTrunk makes a leather "churro" cane that is delicious.

---

4 See Chapter 4 Care and Feeding of Rattan for more info.

5 More on the musicality of canes in Chapter 8

The bull pizzle (stretched dried bull penis) can be shaped into a wonderful, creative leather cane.

Hardwood canes. Caning enthusiasts often overlook hardwood canes. That is a mistake, because hardwood canes offer a distinct range of tonals and frequencies compared to rattan.

The most common woods used are oak, walnut, hickory, pecan, and hard maple. Exotic hardwoods such as zebrawood, bloodwood, paduk, purpleheart, cocobola, and wenge cost more but offer beautiful grain patterns, greater natural color and tonal variety.

Softer hardwoods should be avoided, and all conifer softwoods should be avoided such as pine, fir, spruce and cedar.

The process of making a hardwood cane is straightforward. You can either lathe a dowel rod or buy a hardwood dowel rod that's already turned to the desired diameter and length. Sand the ends to round them. Hand oil, stain, or polyurethane the dowel, and a hardwood cane is born. Designing a handle requires time and craftiness, so the type of wood, diameter, length, and design of the handle all factor into the cost of a hardwood cane from an exotic hardwood cane maker (such as Dex).

B. Rods. Rods resemble canes, but are made from artificial materials. The extent of these materials is almost infinite. I offer here some of the most common types used to get the creative juices flowing.

Rubber. Rubber rods look like canes and hurt like a son of a bitch. Very stingy!

Metal. Metal rods can be made from most metals, including aluminum, steel, copper, and iron. They can be solid or hollow, like an arrow.

Fiberglass. Fiberglass rods are very stingy, flexible, and transfer energy very well. But be careful, as they can break more easily than other rods.

Delrin. Polyoxymethylene (POM) is a highly crystalline engineered thermoplastic or high-performance acetal resin that is durable, stiff, and has dimensional stability. Sounds like it would make an excellent rod for caning, and it does!

Acrylic vs Polycarbonate. Both are dimensionally stable thermoplastics. They have excellent impact resistance. The key difference between polycarbonate and acrylic is that polycarbonate is almost unbreakable, whereas acrylic can be broken if a high force is applied. Polycarbonate is more expensive than acrylic. Acrylic rods are a good alternative because they are not easily breakable and are easy to maintain.

Graphite. Graphite rods are lighter than those made from bamboo or rattan. Graphite is wonderful if used with finesse and skill when caning. The warning on graphite is that it is prone to breaking or the rod snapping under force.

There are, without a doubt, other materials that can be used as a cane. Explore, use your imagination, experiment, and have fun.

Chapter 2
The Crown Jewels

MY SET OF Crown Jewels has a fascinating origin story. They are a fantastic set of canes crafted by Whypdancer at Canes4Pain, each a unique piece of fine art, BDSM-style.

The Crown Jewel canes have deep roots in House Mermaid. House Mermaid was a leather house in upstate NY that served as my home, along with my 24/7 submissive at the time. With the help of a 17-person extended leather family, we built a 2,500-square-foot dungeon space over the summer and fall of 2001.

For over six years, House Mermaid hosted monthly play parties and educational events. The events at the House were always free of charge. They were potlucks, and the only admission fee was the agreement to be discreet. What happened in the House stayed in the House and was never to be discussed outside it.

Over the years, as guests visited and saw the mermaid theme, they would bring me mermaid figurines as gifts. I would place the mermaids on the mantle above the fireplace for display, so that as guests returned, they would see their gifts prominently displayed.

When House Mermaid was disbanded in 2007, I selected my favorite mermaids and sent them to Whyppie, along with 100 feet of custom braided poly rope made for House Mermaid by Rainbow Rope. This rope was royal blue and turquoise with red speckles.

Whyppie spent a significant portion of her spare time unwinding the rope to incorporate it into the handle patterns of the first-generation mermaid canes that she dubbed the Girls.

No one should have only one cane. Canes represent a broad spectrum of sensations and thus come in many sizes, shapes, and lengths. Essentially, the Girls consisted of one of each type of Malacca premium grade rattan crown jewel cane that Whyppie was making at the time. They are a full orchestra, if you will, of canes.

The second generation of the Girls was actually born in 2001, before the first generation, when I bought my first canes from Hanson Paddle. I purchased three raw rattan canes of varying thicknesses, all of which were 30" long.

In that initial cane purchase, there were two baritone canes that were thicker and thuddier than the other one. A strike with the baritone canes produced a wonderful tonal. Throughout my early years of caning, I would start by warming up with these canes.

When I received the first generation set of the Girls, the bass cane in that set replaced the Hanson raw rattan baritone canes in my toy bag, and they were retired to sit in the corner of my home arsenal for many years. Every time I saw them, they brought back good memories, and I missed playing with them.

In the meantime, Whyppie had come up with some new cane designs that I didn't have in my set. There were orchestra pieces available to add to my ensemble! I sent her the two baritone "sticks" and commissioned a second generation of mermaid canes. We agreed to deviate from the original design, allowing Whyppie's artistic creativity to take over in creating this second generation of the Girls. In addition to the two baritone canes, the set included a whangee cane (rattan with the bark and joint knots left on it) and a Sanibel Island beach cane (a sand-coated rod).

The Girls, to this day, have incredible tonals and energy. They are irreplaceable pieces of BDSM art, but are uniquely functional in play, as nothing I own has these tonals.

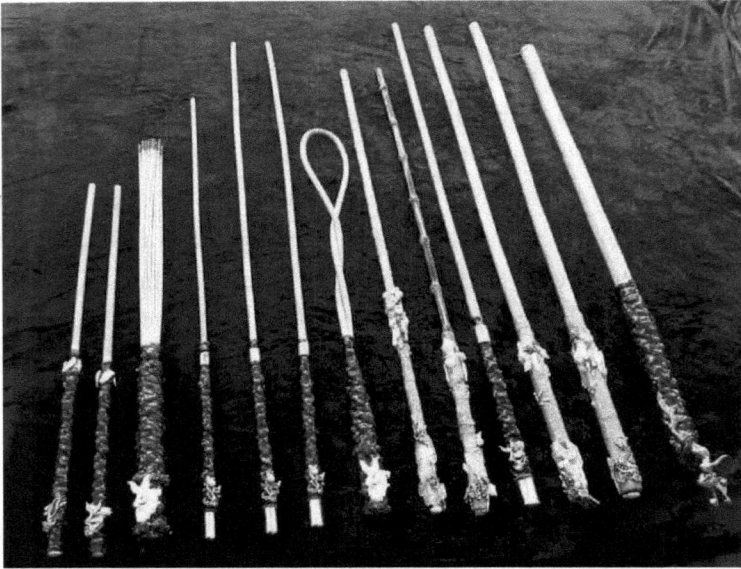

The Girls: Mermaid canes, Crown Jewel canes made by Canes4Pain.

Chapter 3
Pervertibles Morphing into Canes

A PERVERTIBLE IS something intended for a practical vanilla use that, when the kinky eye spots it, the light bulb goes on in the head of the kinky person and they say, that would make a great ____ - fill in the blank.

The pervertibles described in this chapter are vanilla items that can be made into, or are already, great rods or canes. In many cases, because they are artificial, they are rods. While the pervertibles described here make excellent canes or rods, these are not by any means all-inclusive. This chapter aims to share practical ideas and encourage readers to be on the lookout for their own pervertibles.

Garden Shop Bamboo. Often, you will find a rack of bamboo poles of various lengths to be used as garden stakes, trellises, frames, etc. After reading chapter 1, everyone is familiar with my perspective on using bamboo for canes. If it is thick and sturdy enough to use without risk of breaking, it can be perverted and fashioned into a cane. The garden shop—or, if you are lucky enough to live in Florida, a bamboo farm—is an excellent place to source bamboo for use as a cane.

Fishing Rods. In the past, fishing rods were made from bamboo and steel. You might still find a bamboo or steel fishing rod at a thrift shop, someone's curb alert, or garage sale. However, the modern fishing rod is typically made from fiberglass, carbon fiber, or graphite fiber. Graphite fiber is stronger than carbon fiber, so we can narrow this discussion to primarily fiberglass and graphite rods.

The first section of the rod already has a ready-made handle and will likely be well-balanced, as it is made for bait casting. The metal section connecting the tapered end of the first rod section to the second rod section, which extends to the tip, may need to be cut off, sanded, and sealed. This might mean sealing it with marine varnish or tool dip to prevent the rod tip from cutting the caning bottom if the rod tips them in play.

The first section, featuring the fishing rod handle, will be thicker because the butt end is designed for comfort in the hand and is tapered to approximately half the length of the original fishing rod. Overall, this pervertible will be a thicker diameter rod.

The second section of the rod, which ends with the fishing tip/eye, is tapered to a much thinner tip. Thinner is stingier, but this second section is also much more flexible.

The second section will require a handle to be added to it. It is helpful if done in a way that balances the thinner rod. This type of fishing rod, pervertible, can be made more durable and better balanced by adding a rubber cork to the handle end.

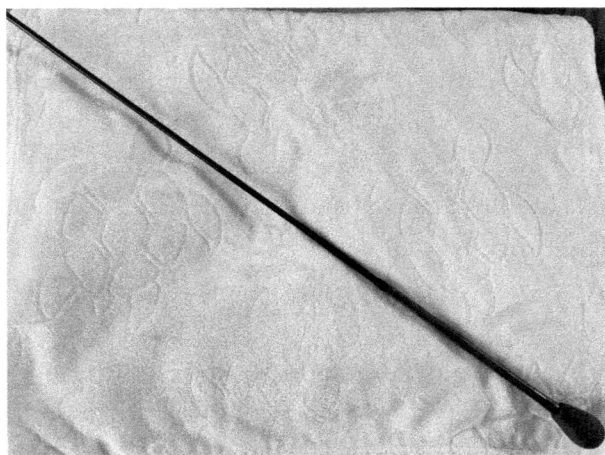

Fiberglass cane made from a fly fishing rod.

Golf Clubs. Antique golf clubs were made out of bamboo or ash wood. You can find these at antique stores. Instead of using this type of older golf club for golfing, consider converting it into a cane.

Living in Florida, I often notice golfers discarding entire sets of golf clubs. The beauty of the set of pervertible golf clubs I acquired is that the irons have steel shafts, while the woods are a combination of graphite and fiberglass, allowing me to have a wide variety of rods.

Modern golf clubs' shafts are made out of carbon steel, stainless steel, graphite, and fiberglass. The handles are perfect for canes. Cut the club's head off and round the sharp edges. Then I recommend dipping them in tool dip.

Cut them to your preferred length, but if you aim to fine-tune the balance, tonal, or vibration frequency of the energy they transmit, I recommend cutting off the head. Hit the rod on the heel of your hand and feel the tonal. Cut off 1/4" at a time and repeat, searching for the tonal that gives the cane the best balance and best vibration when it strikes. You will find the sweet spot of each rod, which is the point at which to stop, round the end, and apply a finish of tool dip to the end.

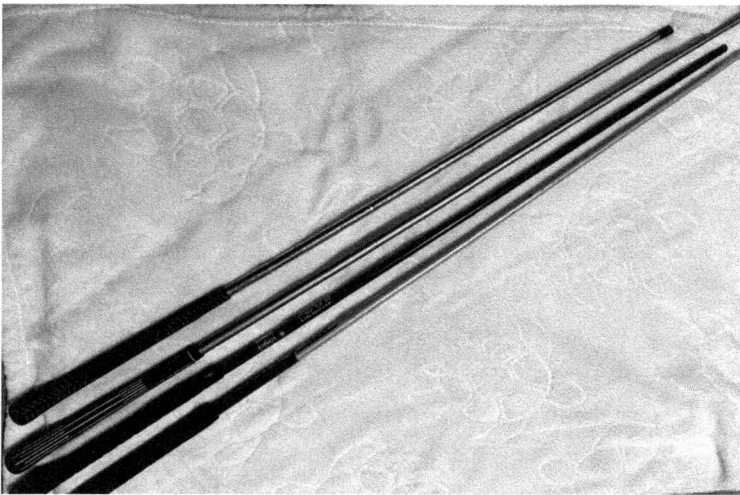

Golf club canes.

Pig Pokers. A pig poker is a carbon-steel rod completely coated in tool dip. It features a handle grip and is used to poke or herd pigs, moving them from one pen to the next.

Pig pokers can be found in agricultural stores. One of your favorite stops will become a Tractor Supply, Rural King, or Agri Supply. Maybe you won't end up with a pig poker, but a stroll around looking for pervertibles usually yields some clever new toy.

The pig poker is heavy and thuddy, with an excellent tonal. It generally surprises anyone who feels it on their bottom.

Arrows. Arrows made from aluminum, carbon fiber, and fiberglass make great play rods. I bought my aluminum arrow shaft at Dick's Sporting Goods for $5. It has an excellent tonal quality, and depending on the technique I'm using, it sounds like I'm killing the bottom I'm playing with—but I'm not. Leave the fletching on, and it can then be turned around and used for sensation play. Unlike some of the other pervertible rods, an arrow shaft fits nicely in every cane carrying case. This is one of my favorite rods.

Feather Dusters. Most feather dusters have a shaft of some sort and can be used for sensual caning and sensation play in erotic areas. Years ago, Dollar Tree sold feather dusters that had a cane shaft wrapped in tape. These were a great addition to my cane case, and each became a gift to the caning bottom they were used on, serving as a remembrance to take home. No doubt every time they dusted their home, they could fondly remember the caning scene with me.

Cooking Chopsticks and Mongolian BBQ Grill Chopsticks. Made of wood — sometimes an exotic hardwood like rosewood — these pervertibles make excellent shorties. They can be used for percussion, erotic play, or OTK (over the knee).

Cooking chopsticks generally come in two sizes, with the handle always being thicker than the tip. The tip end is stingier, and the handle end is thuddier. The handle area is often squared, featuring four sides and four rounded edges. Striking with the squared handle edge will create a different sensation than striking with the rounded edge.

Hardwood Dowels. Home Depot, Lowes, and other hardware stores are sources for dowel rods in different diameters. Be careful in your selection of these for pervertibles as some dowel is made from pine and softwoods. However, walnut is a common dowel material and with a little sanding and sealing becomes a wonderful hardwood pervertible.

Chapter 4

Care and Feeding of Rattan

RATTAN IS A porous vine-like plant that, when straightened and dried, makes the most wonderful canes. However, like any natural material, it will dry out and become brittle over time. It will also lose some of its flexibility and agility. A cane that is not given any attention will become brittle and prone to breaking.

Think of rattan as a wick in a kerosene lamp. The oil will creep up and saturate the wick, keeping it ready to light and burn. Rattan will absorb whatever liquid it is placed in.

Conditioning rattan is simple. Find a container with a narrow diameter that is deep enough to hold ½ to ¾ of the cane, and also able to hold liquid. I like using a three-inch PVC pipe capped on one end. These are found at a hardware store or a store like Home Depot.

Next, take a web-style lawn chair and put the PVC pipe between the webbing so the webbing holds it upright. Acquire a pint of raw linseed oil and pour it into the PVC container you made. Note: Raw linseed oil can be messy, so it's best to do this outdoors or in a garage where any spills won't be a big deal. Place your canes in the PVC container with linseed oil overnight, then remove them and wipe them clean thoroughly the next day. They are now conditioned and ready for play.

*Setup for conditioning canes
with raw linseed oil.*

Freshly conditioned canes should only be used outdoors or in a Dexter room or uncured oil will get on floors, walls and the ceiling. Cast off is a bitch whether oil or blood. Let the raw linseed oil cure for at least a few weeks. Do not carry them in a toy bag with other toys until they have fully cured.

Rattan that has been sealed with marine varnish cannot be conditioned this way unless the varnish is removed from the tip end of the canes. This can be done by sanding the tips until the varnish is removed. The shaft of the cane can remain varnished, and the linseed oil will wick up the porous cane, conditioning it.

Climate and humidity will determine how often canes need to be conditioned, or, as I like to say, given a drink of raw linseed oil to keep them fresh and lively. Linseed oil will wick up the cane a few inches. Get as much of the cane as possible submerged in linseed oil without ruining the cane's pretty handle. As a rule of thumb, give them a drink every six months or so, regardless of where you live.

Acquiring raw linseed oil is no longer as easy as it once was. A few decades ago, every hardware store carried raw linseed oil. Nowadays, the only linseed oil available in most hardware stores is boiled linseed oil. Do not use boiled linseed oil. While it contains additives that speed the drying time of the oil, these additives are toxic. You do not want to be doing edge play with an implement sealed with toxic chemicals. Luckily, raw linseed oil can still be found online. Flaxseed oil can also be used.

A pint of linseed oil can last you several years. When you are finished with a conditioning session for your canes and they are freshly seasoned, take a funnel and pour the linseed oil back into its container. Store it until the next conditioning session.

Birch or rattan bundles should be soaked in water before use. The water wicks up into the bundle, keeping it pliable. It also adds some sting to the implement.

Chapter 5
Cleaning Your Canes

In general terms, some rods are porous and some are not; most rods are not and are infinitely easier to clean than canes. Canes are made out of natural materials, and all of them are porous to some degree. Therefore, cleaning canes must be done with purpose. Additionally, play strategies for your personal toy bag and collection of canes factor into cleaning decisions. Play philosophy, whether it be Safe, Sane, and Consensual play (SSC), or Risk Aware Consensual Kink (RACK), or some other acronym that you follow in your dungeon play approach, is yet another factor in the cleaning equation. Let's look at all of this.

SSC Approach to Cane Play.

Cleaning rods and natural canes that have been sealed with marine varnish is easy. Most rods are not porous and can be cleaned to satisfactory sanitary standards; they can be cleaned to meet the SSC play benchmark and can be used between caning bottoms.

Rods are the easiest to clean and sanitize. Use a hospital-grade cold sterilant, such as Cavicide, or a germicidal/virucidal/bactericidal agent. Read the label for processing times, as most have one (usually 3-5 min). Then, clean the agent off with isopropyl or rubbing alcohol. The alcohol will remove any residual cleaner and evaporate, leaving no residue. Do not put a damp cane back in its carrying or storage case until it has dried completely. I consider this approach acceptable for SSC play.

Most natural canes are porous, and unless sealed with varnish or polyurethane, their porosity can create a potential source of contamination from blood and bodily fluids. Due to its porous nature, a natural cane such as rattan cannot be cleaned with 100% confidence to a sanitary acceptable standard under SSC parameters.

In my opinion, if a natural cane is used to break skin and becomes blood contaminated, or if the cane is used for erotic play and becomes contaminated with bodily fluids, then that cane should be gifted to the caning bottom, as it cannot be 100% confidently cleaned.

Several approaches may be used for SSC play with natural canes. One involves the cane bottom who enjoys unvarnished canes. They own their own canes and request that the caning top use those canes on them during the scene. That way, those canes have only ever been used on the cane owner.

Another approach would be for the caning top to use a new cane on the caning bottom, negotiate an SSC scene, and then gift the cane to the bottom as a token after the scene concludes. Yet a third approach would be for the cane top to use a new cane during the scene, clean it using the procedure described above, and then place it in the cane case where RACK canes are kept.

RACK Approach to Cane Play.

The RACK approach to rods and sealed natural canes involves continuing to clean fastidiously before and after each caning scene, and using the cleaning methods described for SSC play.

For natural canes that are unsealed or have only been conditioned with raw linseed oil, or that are sealed with wax, risk-aware consensual kink is actually the negotiated reality. The caning bottom is informed about how the canes have been used and that they have been cleaned with a hospital-grade antibacterial/antiviral cleaner, then with isopropyl alcohol. Unsealed rattan canes are no more porous than leather implements. Chemicals and alcohol will degrade the rattan. Canes should be reconditioned after this type of cleaning. The caning bottom must realize that, even with this attention to detail and cleaning process, there is no 100% guarantee that the canes are not contaminated. They also agree to play with said canes, being fully aware of the risk, however slight.

The caning bottom may ask if they can clean the canes before their caning scene. That way, the caning bottom can be assured that the canes are clean to their satisfaction.

Chapter 6

Don't Break Your Cane

CANES COST MONEY. Conditioning and taking good care of your canes are the first and most important factors in not breaking a cane. However, canes can and do break. Even rods, depending on the material and thickness, can break.

Canes are made to transfer energy. They are made to strike something resembling human muscle and tissue. They are not made to whip wildly in the air to see how much wind noise they can make or to show off. Whipping a cane in the air to create a windy sound leaves the energy generated by the cane nowhere to go.

When a cane strikes a butt, the energy is transferred from the cane to the buttocks, and neutrality is restored to the cane. When a cane is whipped through the air, it flexes, and the chance of breaking it around the pivot point above the handle increases greatly. In 26 years of caning, the only cane ever broken out of my cane set was broken this way. Predictably, it broke right above the handle.

Wrapping is the second easiest way to break a cane. Wrapping is a result of poor form and technique in caning, unless done intentionally. It is done by the caning top being too close to the caning bottom, given the length of a particular cane that is being used. The cane strike extends beyond the target zone and wraps around the body part being caned.

Often, the wrapped cane strike leaves a small dot on the far side of the target area or body part, away from the top doing the caning. The result of wrapping is that the cane tip becomes over-flexed, which can cause it to break. Do not be surprised if the last two to four inches of the cane break if your form is poor and you are wrapping the caning bottom. If this happens, sand off and round the broken tip of the now-shorter cane and continue using it, but pay attention to proper form and technique.

Hardwood canes come in a broad spectrum of varieties. Some hardwoods have distinct wood grain patterns, while others have difficult to define patterns. Examine the variety and grain pattern of your cane. "With the grain" is the weakest side of a round piece of wood. "Against the grain" is its strongest side. Think of a wooden cane as a tiny wooden baseball bat. A wooden bat, when manufactured, has a "brand" stamped on the "with the grain" side, so when the bat brand is held up and the bat is swung horizontally, the ball most likely will be contacted by the bat against the grain on its strongest side. This reduces the chance of the ball breaking the bat.

If a hardwood cane strike occurs using the against-the-grain side, there is less chance of breaking the cane, as this is its strongest side. However, if the cane strike occurs along the with-the-grain side, it is more likely to break depending upon how hard the cane strike is. Look carefully at your hardwood canes and find the against-the-grain side. Using a permanent marker mark both sides of the with-the-grain side of the hardwood cane with a dot. Hold it up perpendicular to the cane strike. This will orient the against-the-grain side of the wood in the same vector as the cane strike and lessen the chance of breaking your cane.

Do not strike any of your canes on any hard or firm surface of a piece of dungeon equipment—practice using a soft pillow.

Finally, please do not break a cane and ask the cane vendor to replace it. A top breaking a cane is not the fault of the cane maker. Canes are not indestructible, and sometimes they will break for no other reason than years of love and use in the dungeon. Support the cane vendors in your region. Do not break your canes, but if one breaks, have another readily available.

Chapter 7
Introduction to Caning Techniques

CANING TECHNIQUES ARE the heart and soul of this book. During the discussion on techniques, I will also introduce the ensemble of canes.

Canes come not only in different materials, but also in different lengths, thicknesses, or diameters. Most canes are measured in millimeters of thickness. Still, there is inconsistency within the cane makers' guild, as the larger diameter canes often revert to the American measurement system of inches or fractions of an inch.

But the point is, a caning enthusiast needs a full orchestra of canes to play with, as each cane represents a different instrument within the orchestra of caning play. Each cane will have a different frequency range of vibrations, energy, and tonals to carry deliciously to the cane bottom. Every top should indeed have at least one cane in their toy bag. However, it is equally valid that any top who truly loves caning will have more than one cane in their arsenal.

Some of the canes that I will discuss will be capable of all of the techniques. Some of the canes will not be usable for some of the techniques. Some of the techniques cannot be used with some of the canes. Some techniques will be optimized with certain canes, and while they can be used with other canes, the results will not be as rewarding.

Some rods and sealed canes can be used on certain parts of the body and can become contaminated with bodily fluids. Some canes provide beautiful tonals and, because of their conditioned natural nature, transmit excellent vibrations. If these canes are to be used on multiple people they should not be used where they could be contaminated with bodily fluids.

Some canes can produce bass notes and warm up the heart chakra, but are incapable of making a soprano note. Other canes not only produce soprano tones, but elicit matching soprano notes from the caning bottom closely following a strike. Some canes are simple, straightened pieces of rattan. Some canes are beautiful works of BDSM fine art.

What, then, do I recommend for a starter set of canes? Think of a starter set as a quartet and not the whole orchestra. In a mixed voice quartet, you need a bass (7/8-1 1/4"), a tenor (5/8-3/4"), an alto (1/2"), a soprano (3/16-3/8"), and they should be 24"-30" long. Beginners should start with 24" rattan or hardwood canes. As one becomes more accomplished, 30" and 36" can be added. Of course you could go straight to a set of 30" and choke up while learning.

Begin with inexpensive raw rattan, as it is less dense and more forgiving as you learn to strike with it. Once the skill level has improved, condition it by soaking in raw linseed oil overnight. This will season your rattan.

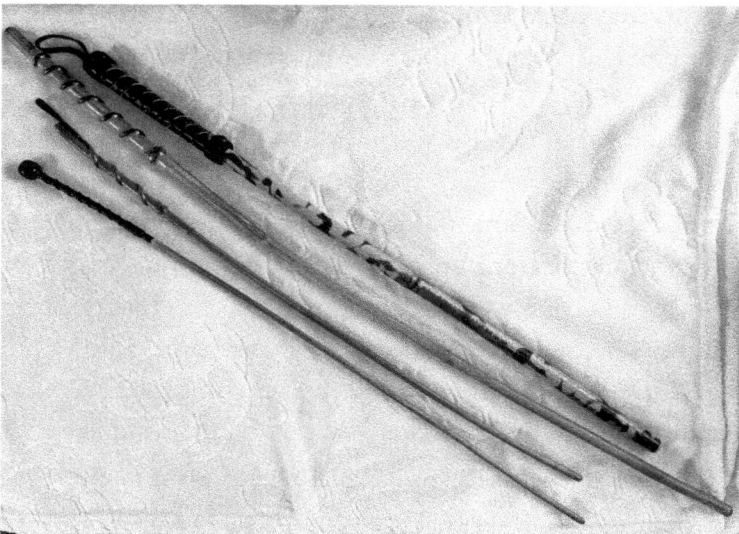

Starter set: The Quartet.

Now that you have read the introduction to canes and you have your quartet starter cane set, let's begin looking at a wide variety of techniques to use with those canes.

A. Warmup.

With any impact play, a good warm-up is essential. Of course, there are circumstances in which specific types of caning can occur without a warm-up (e.g., punishment, corporal, or cold canings). But the best way to a great caning scene is with a deliberate, lengthy warm-up of the skin on all areas to be caned. This warmup is intended to awaken the skin and muscle tissue. Done correctly, it will invigorate and raise the skin temperature to a level noticeable by touch.

Touch the skin before beginning the warm-up to establish a baseline. Then start warming up the skin with light strokes. Every few minutes, check the skin temperature by touching it. Within 5-10 minutes, the skin should be prepared for a great cane scene. Warming up the skin increases circulation, enhances its flexibility, and prepares it to withstand heavier strikes.

Skin color does not always indicate skin temperature. There is a broad spectrum of skin colors and tones that do not reflect the skin's temperature as it warms. Touch is the best hands-on indicator that the skin is warming properly and is ready to be caned.

What can be used for the warm-up? Well, actually, almost anything will do. A bare hand for light spanking, a flogger, or literally anything that can be used to warm up for an impact play scene can be used to warm up before a caning scene. But the caning purists will want to warm up with a cane. What cane should you use for warm-up? Any cane in the starter quartet can be used for warm-up. However, remember that thinner will be stingier, and thicker will be thuddier.

Begin with the thickest cane, as it will be the thuddiest. The goal is to warm up the skin, not to leave marks. Marks come much later and depend upon consent and negotiations. A thick cane will produce deep, heavy tonals. It will translate slow frequencies and begin to awaken the chakra receiving the stroke. At the same time, it will warm up the skin.

A variety of the strokes taught in the sections that follow can be used, but it is important to realize that, for warm-up, these are partial strokes. I like to use tapping and brushing for warm-up. Everyone will eventually settle on their own favorite warm-up.

A good warm-up will reduce the chance of marking with the cane. There is never any guarantee in a caning scene that the bottom will not receive any marks. I would not recommend negotiating "no marks" in any caning scene, as there is such a broad spectrum of skin tones and levels of leather skin depending upon the regularity of play some bottoms may receive. Having said all of that, a good warmup ensures proper preparation for a proper caning, and the results the following day will assuredly be less evident than if there were no warmup.

B. Tapping.

Tapping is typically a partial stroke. However, it can be done with a wide range of intensities. The tapping rate can be varied, but it generally follows a quick cadence, and as a result, even with partial strokes, it tends to build energy.

Tapping, when used as a warm-up stroke, will quickly raise skin temperature. Or if done after a warmup as part of play, it will build energy in the targeted strike zone to a point that can be a slow buildup, a ramp-up, or even a crescendo.

The handhold for tapping is a handshake grip, and the cane strike is a tap of the skin in the target area. Taps, on a spectrum scale, can range from light to heavy. The sensations created by the taps vary depending on the cane selection and differ according to the rod used.

This simple stroke has so many variations and possibilities. If done very lightly, it is almost a ghost stroke; if done heavily, you might be playing a bass drum. Taps can be done on nearly any fleshy part of the body as partial strokes.

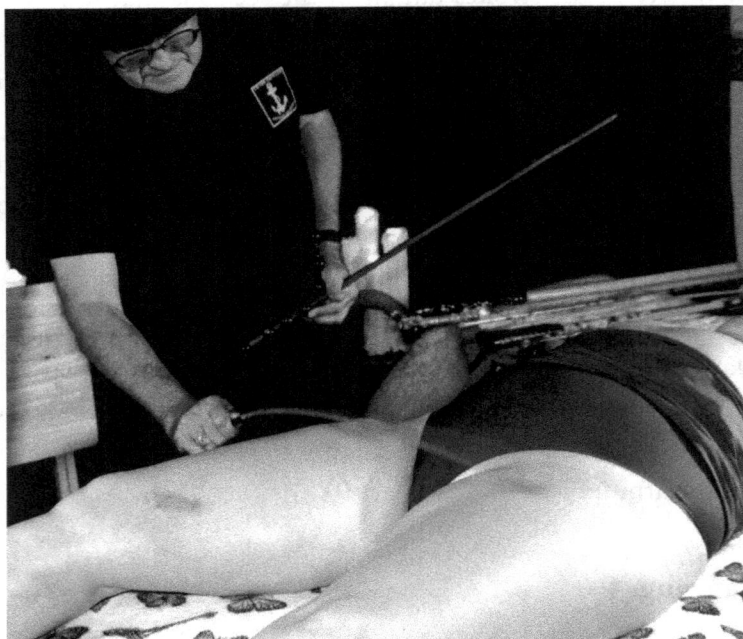

Tapping. Where wrist is lower than cane finish point, lower fulcrum using flexibility of the cane to rapidly tap.

C. Backstop.

Backstop is a technique that involves the non-dominant hand, or the hand not being used to hold the cane. It serves several purposes.

One of the most obvious uses of the backstop technique is that it allows the cane to be stopped on recovery and the direction to be changed for a subsequent strike. When playing with the music, it enables rhythmic caning to fast music without increasing the number of strikes, because the sound the cane makes when it hits the backstop (the other hand) replaces one of the beats in the music, keeping the cane's sound in time with the music.

In contrast, when using a backstop, the actual cane strikes are on every other beat. The distance the backstop hand is held away from the strike zone determines how far the cane must travel to complete a backstop cycle. This can increase or decrease the frequency of the cane strike depending upon the distance the backstop hand is from the strike zone.

A backstop, if done thoughtfully, will give the cane top direct feedback on how much energy is being exchanged by the cane. This is done by trying to hit the backstop with the same amount of energy as the hit in the target zone. The intensity of the cane hitting the backstop is adjusted to imitate the intensity of the cane striking the bottom.

An added input is provided when the body language is read in direct relation to the feel of the cane into the backstop hand. Another input can be to ask the bottom what they feel on a Likert pain scale of 1 to 10.[6] That direct feedback provides a correlation to the energy and feel in the backstop hand.

This is a very valuable technique to use during warmup and is excellent as a modification to the tapping stroke. It is also helpful as a variation to return to as a change-up between some of the more intense strokes. The backstop also introduces sound energy, doubling the cane's sound and adding to the dungeon's ambiance. Backstop introduces matching energy into the cane top. It allows the cane top to share in the energy of the scene as it directly connects that energy between the top and the bottom.

On analysis, it completes an energy cycle through the chi of the cane top and the chi of the cane bottom. How is this possible? Well,

---

6 A Likert pain scale is a subjective tool, where 0 is "no pain" and 10 is "worst imaginable pain," adapting this to negotiations before play and check-ins during play allows the cane top to connect with the pain level, energy, and endorphins the bottom is feeling. The core idea is quantifying subjective pain.

every cane naturally has two ends: the striking end and the handle end. But a cane is also an energy stick. When a strike occurs, that energy not only transfers into the cane bottom, but the cane vibration and frequency also send energy up the striking hand into the cane top's heart chakra.

When the backstop hand is used, energy flows up the other arm into the caning top's heart chakra, energizing that chakra from both sides. Energy is literally buzzing and flowing back down the caning arm into the cane, delivering more energy and shared chi from the caning top and the caning bottom. There is no way to overemphasize the importance of this technique when used to complement the broad range of available caning techniques.

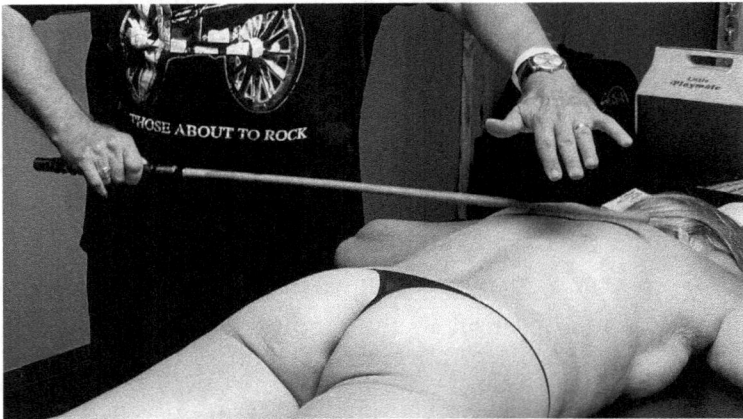

Backstop.

D. Feathering.

Feathering is a descriptive term for this technique, as the cane is lightly brushed across the skin. The hand grip of the cane is the same as for tapping, although other grips can be used as long as the grip does not impede the finesse required of this stroke. One key to this stroke is for the cane to lightly brush across the skin in a passing stroke, producing friction.

The stroke can be done parallel to the skin or in a J-stroke pattern, with the J's hook feathering the skin. While this is a light stroke, it makes a great warm-up stroke. However, please do not abandon it as a caning scene progresses. It is an excellent stroke to use between other, more intense techniques. It provides different sensations and can be used to spread and move energy when used with heavier techniques.

Feathering a target area after a heavy caning can produce chills. It is such a different sensation. Envision creating the feeling of a fluffy feather with a stick. Indeed, it is not a heavy stroke. Think light and airy as you feather your caning bottom.

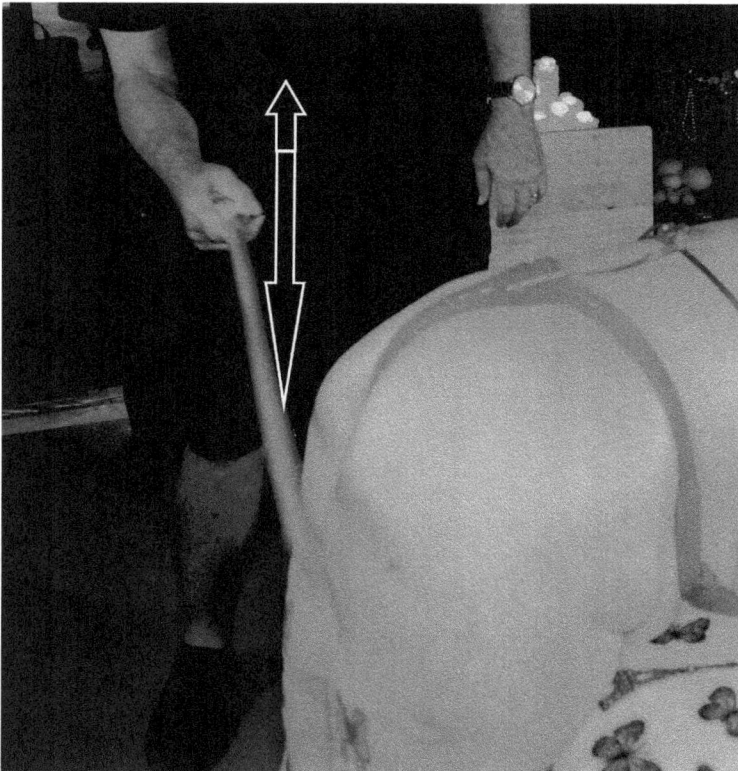

Feathering. Brushing stroke. Vertical up and down creating skin friction with the cane. Horizontal uses a more U shaped stroke.

E. Tipping.

Think of the parts of a cane: there is the handle, the shaft, and the tip. The term tipping has evolved over the decades I've been caning. It can refer to just the very tip of the cane being used, or it can refer to the last 3 or 4" of the cane being used. The tip should be sanded and rounded so that it does not cut anyone on a strike. But the tip itself provides yet another technique.

Striking with just the tip of the cane can be as light as feathering, or it can leave a streak or a mark. Tipping in erotic zones is especially fun. Be sure consent is negotiated before the scene begins if you plan on tipping or actually using any stroke in an erogenous zone. Some bottoms may welcome it, while others may see it as crossing a line.

Tipping can be done on any meaty part of the body. Tipping with the last 3-4" of the cane reminds me of a wizard transferring energy to selected parts of the body. This can be done to energize different parts of the body and is a technique used in free-form caning (more on free-form caning in Chapter 13).

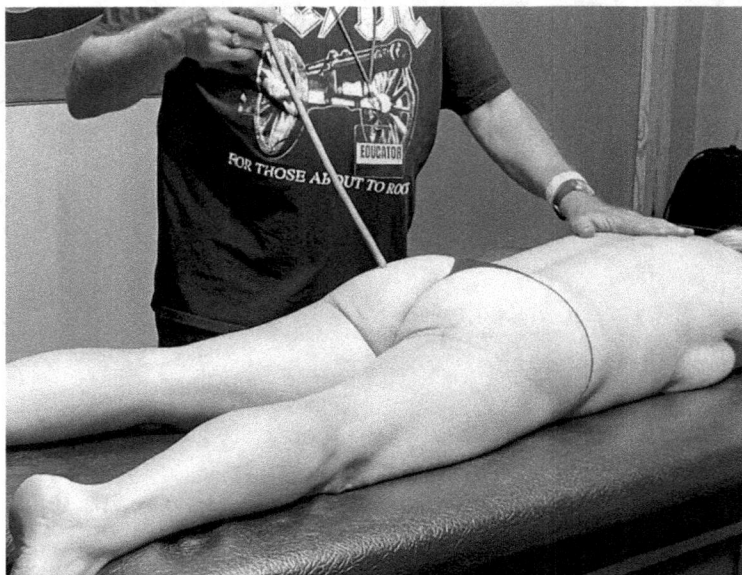

Tipping.

F. Drumming or Percussion.

Percussion can be done using full-sized canes or shorties. A shortie is just what it sounds like. It is a short cane, usually 16-20" long.

Percussion can be done single-handed or with two canes, one in each hand. It can also be done with a birch or rattan bundle, which gives a bit of the feel of a drum brush or rute, sometimes spelled ruthe. A rute is a cane bundle used to play a bass drum – just substitute a butt for the drum.

Percussion can be done in unison or in alternating rhythms and patterns. For those who have actually played drums or taken rudimentary drumming lessons, all of that can apply to drumming with a cane. This is a former high school drummer's chance to put all the things they learned in band to use in an adult, kinky setting.

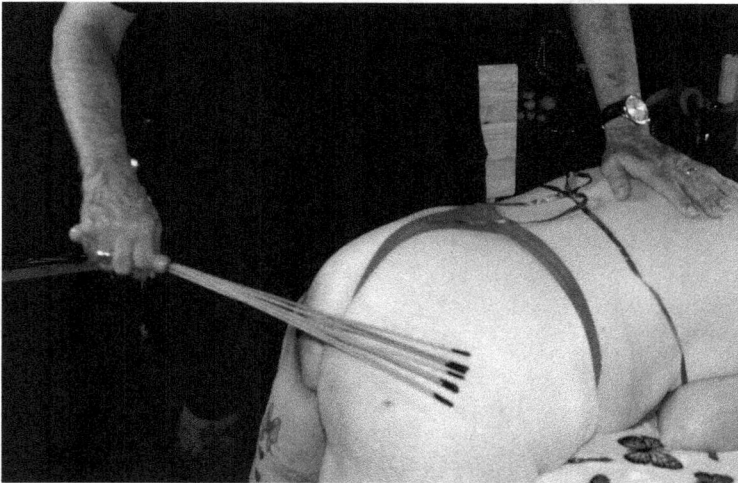

Percussion using a rattan bundle striking
the apple part of the butt cheek.

G. Bouncing.

Bouncing is done with a very specific handhold. The cane is held between the thumb and first finger, forming a pivot point using a pincer grip, and the handle end bounces off the heel of the hand. Gravity and the weight of the cane determine most of the energy of the strike. The heel of the hand can apply energy, speeding up the pivot and increasing the force of the bounce. Think of the cane as being a teeter-totter action in the hand, much as a teeter-totter on a playground. Only now the playground is the caning bottom.

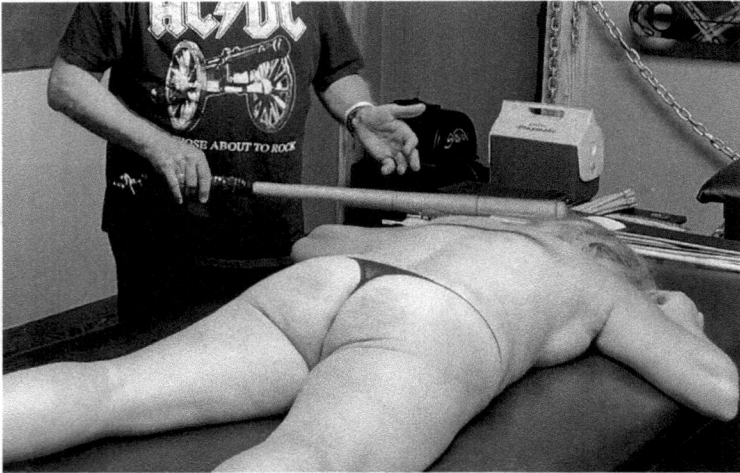

Bouncing technique on the heart chakra.

H. Punching or Whiplash.

Punching is a relatively new technique in my experience, and it evolved from learning whiplash from my friend Gloryus. The technique between the two is the same, but the result from the cane strike is different, and the cane action is different; therefore, the energy transfer is different. Needless to say, the bottom experiences the sensation differently. The size and length of the cane used produce different sensations with the same technique.

To produce the punch technique, a punch, or heavy, concentrated strike, is made with a larger cane. This is easiest to achieve with a 3/4" to 1" thick cane. My preference for this stroke is a 24"-30" long cane. Think of the stroke as hitting with the last ¼ of the cane and placing the fulcrum of the hand/wrist below the strike target.

Begin with a partial punch. Move the punch around between strike zones so the bottom does not know where the next punch is coming. Increasing the punch's strength will result in heavier strikes. The cane will try to settle at the level of the fulcrum point, so adjusting the fulcrum height will change the finish of the cane against the target zone.

Part of this action of the cane is a reflection of the thickness of the cane, as a thinner, more flexible cane would not tend to achieve the fulcrum level. The thinner cane would flex. Care must be taken not to punch too strongly and not break any bones. Stay with meaty, fleshy target areas. Of course, Gloryus might call this technique tipping, as it is similar to her magic cane technique.

Whiplash is the same technique used for a punch, but with a thinner, more flexible cane. The whiplash feels almost like a whip strike, and the action of the cane is much different, even though the top is using the same technique as in punching.

The whiplash is accomplished by lowering the fulcrum (the hand) below the bottom's target area and using the flexibility of the cane to whip the first 1/3 of the cane into the bottom. Cane bottoms have described the sensation as stingy and feeling almost like a whip strike with a singletail.

Whiplash uses the inertia of the cane bouncing off one end of the body to allow it to lay the full length or width of the body and end up striking the meaty cheek. Whiplash can leave whip-like marks. A 30-36" long cane that is thinner and more flexible is best for this technique. Realize that a longer cane is easier to break than a shorter cane, and when using a 36" thin cane, good technique is essential. This is an advanced technique. Beginning cane tops should not try it until they become proficient. This is a great way to break canes mid-shaft. The cane should not break if the technique is applied correctly.

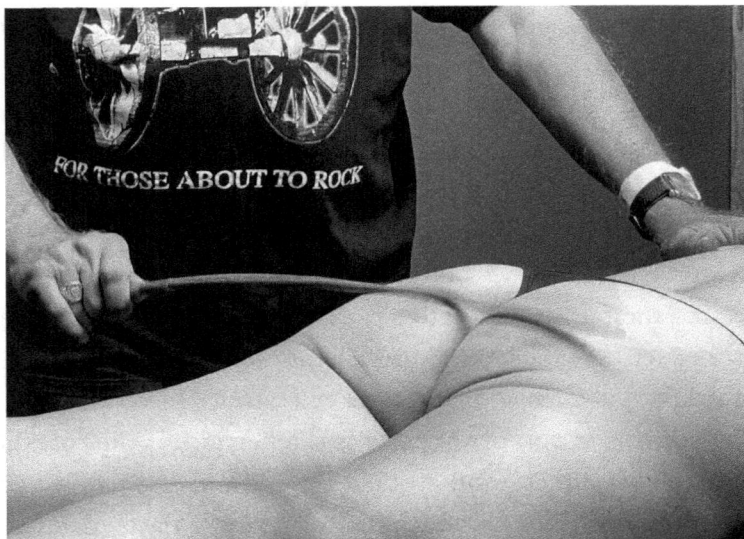

Whiplash.

I. Strike Back.

This stroke, which occurs around the country, is known by different names, but I have always called it strike back. This requires some visualization and imagination. Visualize striking the skin with the cane and, in the instant the cane strikes the skin, pulling it back. Thus, the stroke is a strike-and-back. I have, for years, described this as imagining striking a block of tofu and transferring all the energy in the cane to it without cracking the tofu.

This stroke will rarely leave a mark if done correctly, but it can be intense. It also, when done correctly, makes a very loud slapping sound. This sound varies depending on the thickness of the cane and its material. A fiberglass rod will make an audible thwack. Some might call this stroke a "slap" or "slapping stroke," as its effect is akin to a slap to the skin. This stroke is the seed that grew into the Vegetarian Caning workshop (for those readers who've seen this presentation).

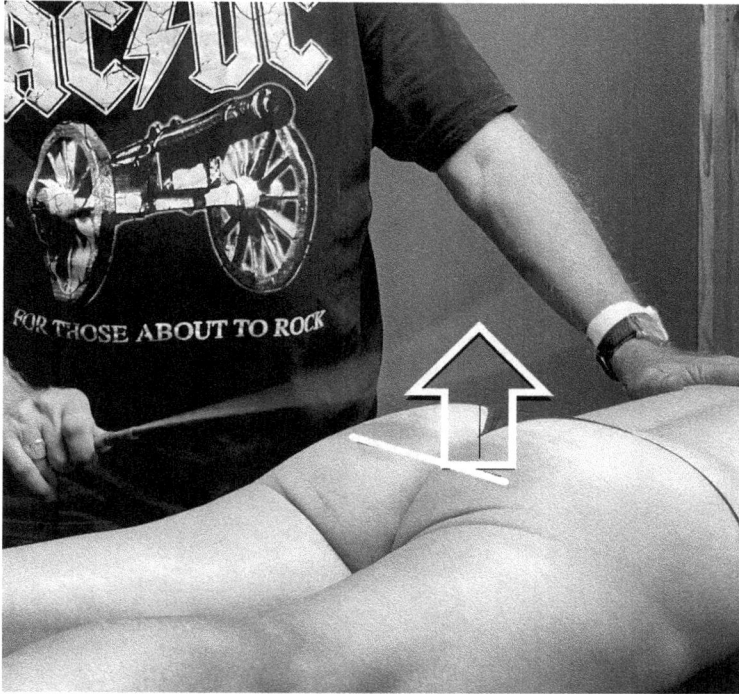

Strike Back.

J. Strike-and-Hold.

Strike-and-hold is an accurately descriptive term for the stroke.

Strike the target zone with the cane and hold it against the skin, allowing all the energy from the cane to penetrate and be absorbed by the body. Hold the cane there and read the bottom's body language. Until the bottom's body language tells you that all of the energy has entered the body and been processed, and the bottom is ready for another strike, do not pick up the cane. Leave it there, pressing into the skin. There is no rush.

Strike-and-hold can be done with partial strokes all the way to a full stroke. This variation illustrates how all of these caning techniques can produce different results.

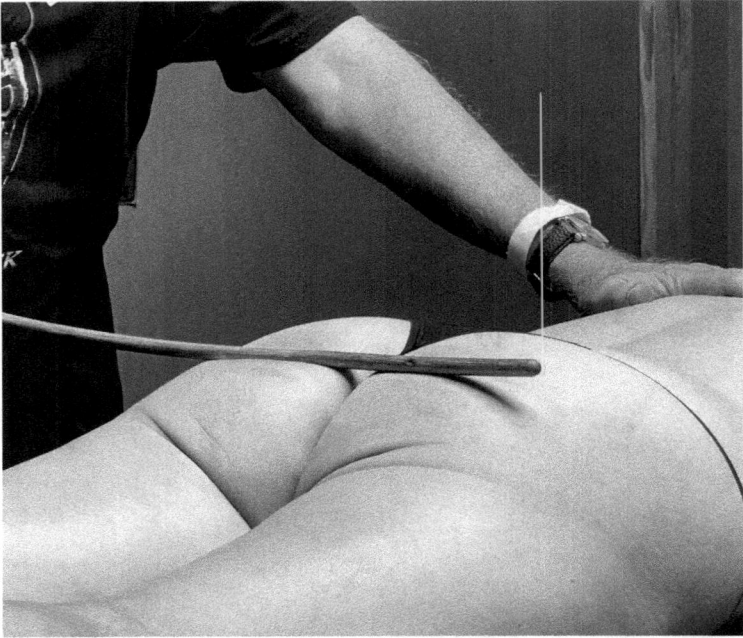

Strike and Hold.

K. Strike-and-Draw.

Strike-and-draw is a very instrumental stroke. Think of a cello or upright bass player drawing a bow across the strings. First, there is a strike, then, instead of holding the cane, it is drawn across the skin as a bow. This spreads the energy out, drags it across, and draws it into the skin and muscle. The draw can be toward the caner or away from the caner. Both would produce similar yet different effects. Just as a bow produces different sounds when pushed as compared to when it is pulled, so too does a cane, providing a subtle variation on the technique.

L. Strike-Through.

Strike-through is a very intense stroke. It can only be done safely with a relatively flexible cane and, therefore, is not recommended as a technique with thicker canes.

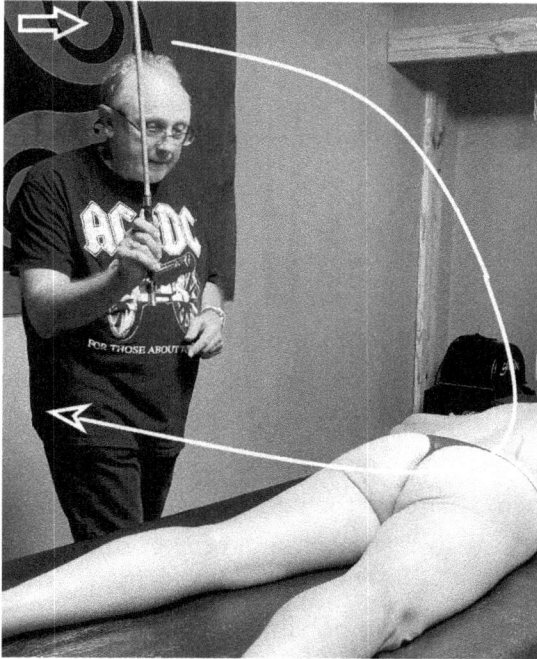

Strike Through.

Visualize a stroke that begins high. The cane is brought down to hit the strike zone, passing through it and finishing on the other side of the bottom. Obviously, the cane is not going to actually pass through your cane bottom. Instead, the force used remains constant *as if* it were meant to pass through to the table. Another way of thinking about it is that the cane makes a complete arc on the stroke, and the middle of that arc is where it hits and flexes, passing through the strike zone. Ensure you have enough room on the windup, strike and follow through to not hit anything unintended.

Strikes from this technique usually leave marks, regardless of how well the bottom is warmed up. This technique also requires the top to read the bottom's body language and to allow the bottom to process the pain from the strike and breathe. Multiple strike-throughs may require pain management techniques (Chapter 16 provides more detail on pain management) to allow the top to work with the bottom in processing the rapidly ramped-up endorphins.

M. OTK and the J Stroke.

OTK, or over the knee, is a play position usually associated with spanking. But spanking can be done in multiple ways: with the bare hand, with a belt or paddle, and yes, with a cane.

A shortie (usually 16-20" long) or, if using a pervertible, the length of a drumstick or cooking chopstick, is perfect for OTK.

The top is sitting comfortably on, perhaps, a chair or a bed, and the bottom lies face down over the top's lap. The striking arm is raised shoulder high and parallel to the floor, and is taken with the cane through a J-shaped stroke finishing on the bottom's buttocks.

There are many ways to utilize this OTK position. All of the strokes described above are possible with a shortie. Feathering, tapping, bouncing, strike-and-hold, strike-and-draw, and strike-through all lend themselves beautifully to this J stroke action.

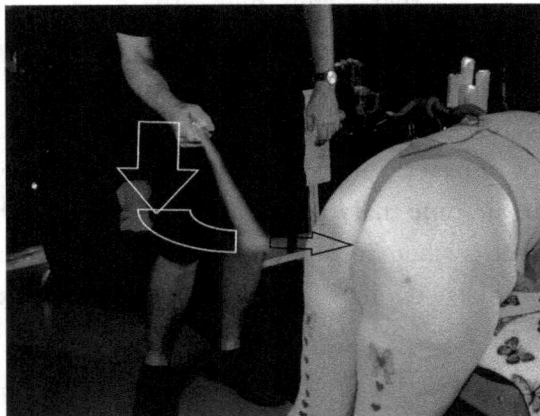

The J Stroke.

N. Off-the-Shoulder.

Off-the-shoulder refers to the resting position of the cane at the start of the stroke. There are multiple ways to swing using an off-the-shoulder technique, and most of them relate directly to the position of the bottom or the type of equipment used in a particular caning scene.

If a bondage table or massage table is used, the cane bottom is lying horizontally, either face up or face down. The top rests the cane on the shoulder of their dominant or striking arm, and the cane is drawn straight down in an arc off the shoulder.

This technique is highly accurate, as it involves a straight downward motion, and the direction can be guided by the thumb of the striking hand holding the cane. Think of the thumb as a pointer identifying the exact location of the cane strike.

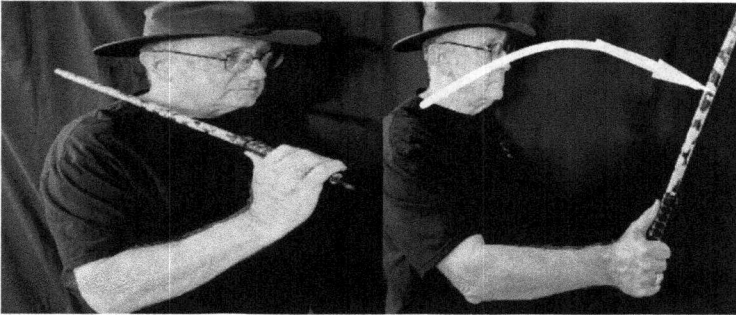

Off-the-Shoulder.

The other off-the-shoulder style originates from the Belgian leather scene and is executed from a standing position. The bottom is standing, either unrestrained or restrained to a St. Andrew's cross. The top is standing parallel to the cross and facing away from it. The cane rests behind the neck and parallel to the shoulders. The top's off-hand is pointed toward the buttocks of the bottom to help guide the stroke. The dominant hand holding the cane is swung off the shoulders in an arc as the top's body swivels to face the cross, providing power to the stroke.

For the Belgian style off-the-shoulder technique, think of the hand holding the cane swinging in an arc to clap the off-hand that is pointing toward the bottom's butt. This stroke takes some practice, but is an excellent punishment stroke, as not only the energy of the cane but also the top's torso, legs, and feet engage the top's core/chi, thereby energizing this stroke.

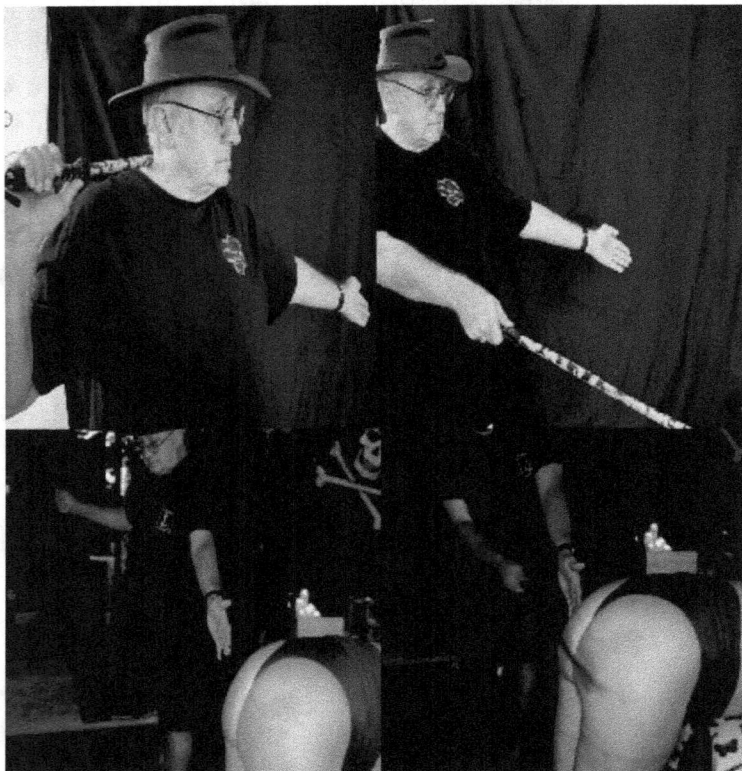

Belgian Off the Shoulder punishment stroke.

O. Two Cane Techniques.

Two cane techniques require, of course, two canes. The canes do not have to be the same diameter or the same length. There are many applications for using two canes. The most obvious is with percussion, which can be done two-handed with shorties. Think of a drummer drumming, and the buttocks are two toms. Two raw rattan canes can be used with beginning tops to speed up and ensure accuracy during the learning process.

Guide rod. Again, this technique requires two canes. Think of one cane as a guide rod. Anchor the guide rod cane with the tip of the cane on or directly adjacent to the location to be struck. Then, with the striking cane, slide the cane down the guide rod until the cane strikes the target very accurately.

This technique can be used even by experienced cane tops when the cane strike requires exceptional accuracy or the target area is very small.

An example might be anchoring on a massage table between the legs and having the guide rod between the minor labia such that the cane hits the mons pubis (fatty tissue area above the pubic bone), or even more precisely, on the clitoris.

Anchoring the guide rod directly below a nipple ensures that the striking cane is going to hit the nipple and nothing else.

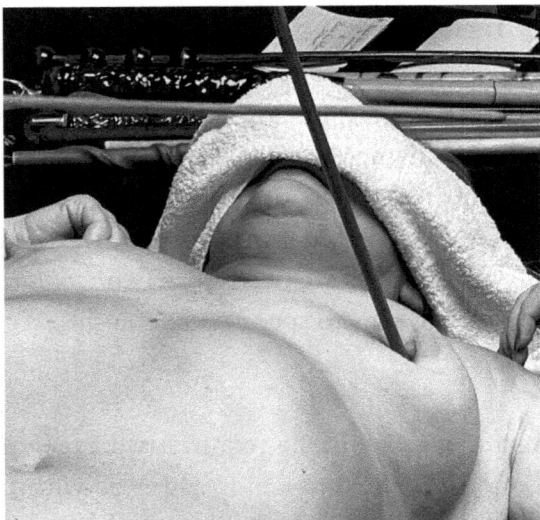

*Two cane technique, guide rod
and striking cane, nipple.*

This same technique can be used in the center of a male's ball sack to ring the bells with a cane strike. As always, remember that if there is a possibility of the guide rod cane coming in contact with bodily fluids, it is advised to use a sealed cane or a rod that is easily cleaned.

Vibration play. This technique also uses a guide rod and a second cane. The guide rod can be used to transfer vibrations or different frequencies to the caning bottom.

The guide rod placement just previously described, between the major labia or splitting the scrotum, is an interesting placement for this technique. If the second cane is used to tap the guide rod, depending upon where it is tapped, it will create a vibration that travels down the guide rod and vibrates the clitoris or the balls. Moving the tapping up or down the guide rod changes the length of the frequency wave, thereby lowering or raising the vibration. Envision turning the guide rod into a tuning fork (more on vibration play in the next chapter). Just as a tuning fork thickness alters the pitch and vibration so also the thickness of the cane used as a guide rod will provide different vibrations.

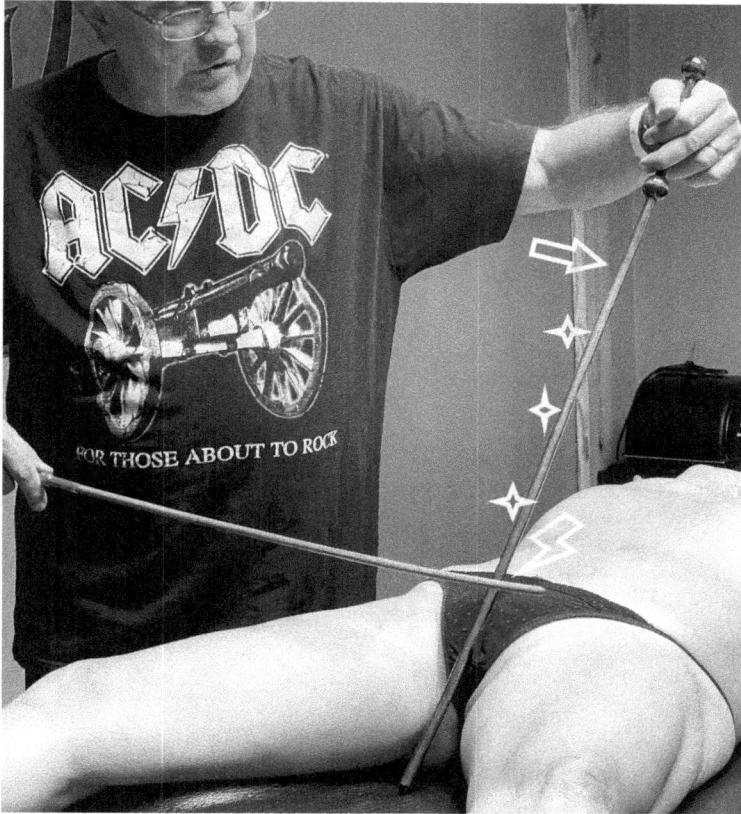

Two cane technique, vibration play.

Bastinado. The two-handed cane technique is ideal for bastinado as exact strikes of the feet are required, and even an experienced cane top can be challenged.

Anchor the guide rod such that the cane strike can be placed precisely on the front arch behind the first metatarsal, for example. Or put the guide rod between two toes so the cane strike occurs directly on a metatarsal pad. Or by using the other side of the guide rod, with the toe pad or toe pads at the exact distance from the toe placement, the toe pad or toe pads can be hit.

Oiling the guide rod allows it to slide smoothly between the toes, creating an interesting sensation all its own.

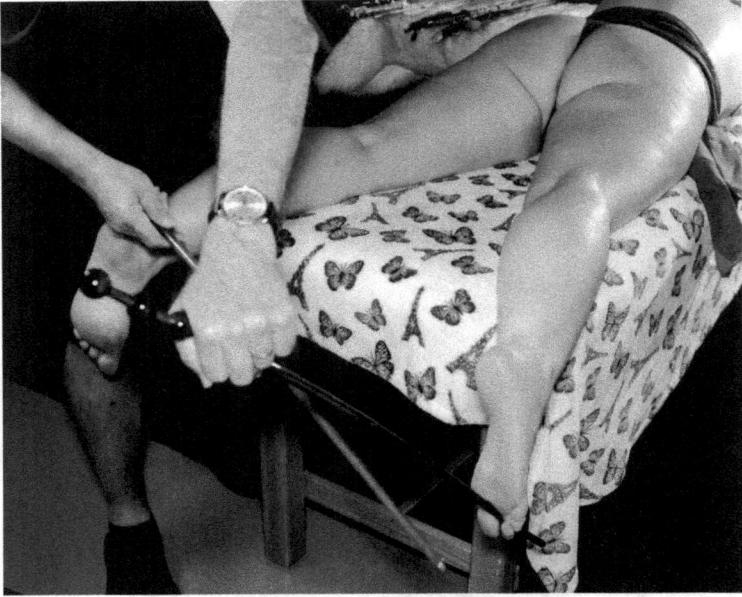

Two cane technique. Bastinado.

Chapter 8

Playing the Cane as an Instrument

THERE ARE SEVERAL aspects behind this idea of playing the cane as an instrument. First, every cane will be different because of differences in diameter, length, handle design, balance, and the density of the material the cane is made of. Whether a natural cane was conditioned and how it was finished is yet another variable. A conditioned cane will be denser, have a different resonance, and carry a different tonal quality than a raw cane. Wet skin or sweat is another variable that will increase intensity.

Think of an individual cane as a type of instrument —a percussion instrument. Each instrument, because every cane is unique, will have nuances because of the variables.

Regardless of their differences, every cane has a natural vibration when it strikes and a natural frequency that vibration makes. Every cane transmits energy through the length of the cane differently and is received differently in different parts of the body.

Every cane bottom is different. And just like a musical performance, every cane scene, even with the same cane bottom, is different. The cane bottom, from one day to the next, may receive and process the energy of the cane differently than the day before.

The Quartet. Everyone needs more than one cane. As stated in the introduction to the chapter on techniques, I recommend having at least four canes that can be thought of as a quartet.

To reiterate, a mixed quartet singing group typically consists of a bass, a tenor, an alto, and a soprano. In the cane quartet, you need a thick cane (a bass) that is 7/8-1 1/4" in diameter; a tenor cane that is ~3/4"; an alto cane that is ~1/2"; and a soprano cane that is ~3/16-3/8".

For the beginner set of canes, start with 24" long canes. By having them all the same length as you are learning, you have eliminated one variable and can focus on playing the bass, tenor, alto, and soprano canes. As your skill improves, you can move up to longer canes. I prefer the 30" length for my quartet.

The quartet of canes will each transmit different energies, and their sensations upon impact will range from thuddy to less thuddy, to stingy and really stingy.

The Orchestra. An orchestra of canes is a full, ongoing collection of canes and rods. Begin expanding on the quartet to include tonals missing, like baritone and second tenor. Add the variable to each thickness of different lengths.

I like 30" long canes as they are longer than 24" but do not require the finesse, good technique, and skill that a 36" long cane requires. The longer and thinner the cane, the easier it is to break, and the more precise your technique must be to wield it without breaking it.

Up to this point, without explicitly stating it, I have been talking about rattan canes. But any natural cane will add an instrument to the orchestra. Thus, hardwood canes provide yet another section of instruments, as there is a spectrum of hardwood varieties ranging from more common hardwoods (such as maple, walnut, cherry, mahogany, hickory, and oak) to exotic hardwoods (including purpleheart, padauk, wenge, tigerwood, and ebony).

The thickness and length of the hardwood canes create another variable in this section of instruments. The main difference between hardwoods is the density and hardness of a particular species. This translates into different tonals and vibrations to the bottom receiving the cane strike.

Leather canes provide yet another section for the orchestra, whether it is green or rawhide that has been wet and twisted to dry in a cane shape, or whether it is a bull penis stretched and dried into a bull pizzle.

Rods will further expand your cane orchestra's offerings, as they offer a variety of materials, including fiberglass, acrylic, Delrin, and even steel and aluminum.

The full orchestra.

Direct play with the instrument. Choosing which instrument in the orchestra to play, at any point in the composition, is influenced by the particular point in the scene at which the decision is made.

One might decide to begin with a bass cane that has deep, thuddy tonals for a warm-up of the heart chakra. The warmup might be alternated between the heart and root chakras, using deep tonals to awaken the chakras' energy and encourage communication up and down the chakra system, employing a tapping or backstop technique.

However, early selection also has other factors at play. Suppose a cane bottom in negotiation has communicated that they don't like thuddy, but they enjoy stingy. One might select an alto cane to warm up with and use a feathering or bouncing technique. For this scene, I would retire the bass and baritone canes and give them a night off.

If negotiations allow for leaving marks and the bottom has indicated a fondness for them, then ramping up with more intense strikes logically occurs with a shorter warm-up period. Learning to play the instruments in a large ensemble orchestra and the selection of techniques are variables in learning to play cane and rod instruments directly.

This discussion could continue through the various transitions of a cane scene and the decision tree each cane top uses to select not only the instrument but also the technique and the intensity of its application at any given point in the scene. But to do that, the book would never have an ending, as the options are endless.

Skill in crafting a good caning scene using a spectrum of orchestra instruments involves factors such as learning how to negotiate a cane scene up front, reading the audience during the composition (the cane bottom), and complementing the energy of the music playing in the dungeon with techniques in direct play that accompany the music rhythmically and at an appropriate energy level. Thankfully, a good caning scene allows the caning top to improvise.

The goal here is to introduce the concepts and get your creativity flowing as you discover your own approach to direct play using the cane orchestra.

Indirect play or vibration play with the instrument. Indirect or vibration play with a cane involves using a two-cane technique. For this, choose a cane that has good vibration and frequency, position it as an anchor cane, and then use another cane that has a lower vibration or frequency (usually slightly thicker than the anchor cane) to strike the anchor cane.

Think of the anchor cane as a neck on an instrument to be played. For every location you strike the neck (anchor cane) with the bow cane (percussion cane), you will create a different frequency or vibration that will carry energy down the anchor cane to the place on the caning bottom where the anchor cane is anchored.

Tapping or striking the anchor cane at different locations alters the vibrations that are carried to the anchored location. Just as a guitarist can do a slide by striking a note on one fret and sliding up to another fret, a caning instrumentalist can strike the anchor cane and slide the percussion cane down the anchor cane's neck to finish at the anchor location.

This is an interesting technique to use when playing with erogenous zones, whether the anchor splits a ball sack and the vibrations chime the bells, or whether the anchor splits the major/minor labia and rests against the clitoris, good vibrations are bound to happen.

The Caning Bottom is an Instrument. The caning bottom anatomically presents as an instrument, and different parts of the anatomy naturally present as certain types of instruments.

The butt cheeks are bongo or tom-type drums. The shoulders and heart chakra area provide entry into the chest cavity, allowing for deep vibrations and responses similar to those of a kettle drum.

Much of playing the caning bottom as an instrument involves reading body language - letting the cane strike bud, burst into bloom, blossom, and begin to wilt before striking that area again. While all of this is happening, tapping and other techniques can be done in different parts of the body.

Often, cane strikes produce stars in the head of the bottom. These shooting stars need time to trail off and dissipate before the instrument can continue to be played. Many songs have rest notes, and the spaces and rest notes are as important as the notes played on the instrument. The rest allows the previous note to be enjoyed and the resonance to carry energy through the body.

Chapter 9

Ramping Up

A GOOD CANING scene is tied to endorphins and the brain's chemistry. There are many ways to ramp up these endorphins. Here are some examples to build upon.

Counting each strike. The caning top can count each strike. Each strike adds energy and increases the endorphin rush. Or, the top can ask the caning bottom to count each strike: one, two, three, four, and so on.

There are different ways to count. A variation on single hit counting would be this: one = 1 hit with the cane. Two = 2 hits with the cane and no rest between the hits. Three = 3 hits from the cane with no rest between hits. Each round in this instance builds the number of strikes, and the energy naturally ramps up.

Increasing the intensity of each strike. This method can be done using most caning techniques.

The first strike is light. The next strike is a little bit harder. The subsequent strike is a little bit harder. Every subsequent strike is a little harder, until finally the bottom's body language communicates that they need time to process the energy. Once the energy has wilted and the bottom has resumed their position to continue, repeat the process. Or shift to a different ramp-up method.

Hitting the same damn spot. Hitting the same damn spot is also a technique that can be used to ramp up. The cane strike does not have to be hard for this technique to be effective because energy pools and is additive. Every strike in the same damn spot (SDS) is building on the previous strike in that same spot. Because a cane strike radiates out every strike in a 4" area will feel like the SDS and will lessen trauma building upon trauma. SDS can be light and still very intense. It can be intense and become even more intense.

Changing the diameter of the cane. A thicker cane is thuddier and has a lower frequency. A thinner cane is stingier and has a higher frequency. Shifting from a thuddy cane to a stingier cane for repeated strikes will have the effect of ramping up.

Removing the rest notes. There are several ways to describe this ramping-up technique. Increasing the frequency of strikes, not allowing the bottom to breathe between strikes, speeding up the rhythm of strikes, removing rest notes, and eliminating recovery time for the bottom; all of these phrases paint a picture of this type of ramp-up.

Chapter 10
Rhapsodic Caning and Music

RHAPSODIC CANING IS rhythmic caning that connects to the music playing in the dungeon during a scene. Any good impact play is connected rhythmically to the music playing in the space. There cannot be enough emphasis on how important music is in a great dungeon setting, but it is right up there with mood lighting.

There are different ways to connect with the music while playing with canes. Rhythm is essential, as is striking on the beat. However, sometimes striking off the beat or syncopating it can be effective. Syncopating should not be done at the detriment of the caning bottom.

I recommend that you do not overuse striking off the beat of the music as a mind fuck. You do not want to break trust with the bottom. Caning is a form of edge play within the world of impact play. It requires a lot of trust on the part of the caning bottom. Do not break that trust; instead, build on it. Build on it by being connected to the music, and let the cane bottom anticipate that the strikes are going to connect closely with the music.

Choosing an element of the music to play along with is one way to connect with it. You can play along with the kick drum in a song. Or you could play along with the bass guitar line. You might switch between the bass line and the melody, or follow the melody in the verse and switch to the kick drum in the chorus—so many options to connect to the music. Let the song speak to you and interact with it.

The choice of instrument can also be a factor in connecting to a part of the song. The top might choose a bass cane for the kick drum part. This deep thuddy cane would easily match up to the deep driving sound of the kick drum.

A baritone or tenor cane might be used to connect to a tom fill. A soprano cane might be perfect for playing along to a top hat rhythm. The snare drum might be calling to a cane bundle, as its sounds are similar. A thin, flexible cane might be perfect to play with a lead guitar solo.

Many of the instruments in the caning orchestra can be matched to those used in the music. A cane, while a type of percussion instrument, is much more. It is a rhythm instrument, a solo instrument, an accompanying instrument, and an ensemble instrument. It can play a wide range of genres, including pop, metal, jazz, bluegrass, rock, and classical. There is literally a cane for every type of music.

Chapter 11

Equipment and Positions

THERE IS A variety of dungeon equipment that complements a caning scene. Positions are often directly related to the equipment used. Additionally, there are general guidelines regarding positions and muscle structure that apply to caning.

If a muscle group is taut, the cane strike will hurt more than if a muscle is relaxed. Often, the position the bottom is in relative to the equipment being used stretches the muscle group. Even though the bottom may be relaxed, the cane strike is going to hurt anyway because of the position of the body on a particular piece of equipment.

For example, caning someone's butt who is standing in front of a St. Andrew's cross with their butt cheeks relaxed is going to hurt less than caning someone bent over a spanking bench with their butt muscles stretched tight, even if they consciously try to relax those muscles - assuming the caning strikes are equal in intensity and the same cane is used for both positions.

Standing. This position complements the use of a St. Andrew's cross, a whipping post, or a chain spider web. Almost any fleshy part of the body facing the caning top can be a target for a partial cane strike. The buttocks and thighs are target areas for more intense strikes.

Prone or Horizontal. This position is complementary to using a massage table, bondage table, or even a bed. It easily accommodates face-up play or face-down play.

This play is logically the most relaxing for the caning bottom. Relaxed is good when caning, as the cane can penetrate more easily to exchange energy than if it has to drive through taut muscle fiber. A relaxed muscle can accept more energy from the cane than a taut muscle can. A tight muscle is almost like armor, but the cane strike will hurt a tight muscle more than a relaxed one.

On All Fours. This position can be achieved with no equipment at all. It can also be accomplished with several different spanking bench designs. A spanking bench allows this position to be achieved while supporting the torso. This enables the caning bottom to relax even though their bum is bent over and presented for caning.

Over the Knee (OTK). This position is usually accomplished with the caning top seated in a chair or on a bench, and the caning bottom bends over the top's knee. There are variations of this position, and the bottom can bend over one knee or both knees of the caning top. Typically, a short cane or shortie is used for this type of caning.

Bent Over. This position can also be achieved without equipment, as a flexible caning bottom can bend over and grab the back of their knees. However, equipment makes this easier, and a wide variety of furniture can be used to accomplish this.

Bent over works well with the torso lying on a bed, massage table, or bondage table. Other ideas include bending the cane bottom over the arm of a stuffed couch, recliner, or a kitchen counter. Caning does not always have to be done in a dungeon (evil grin). It can be spontaneous.

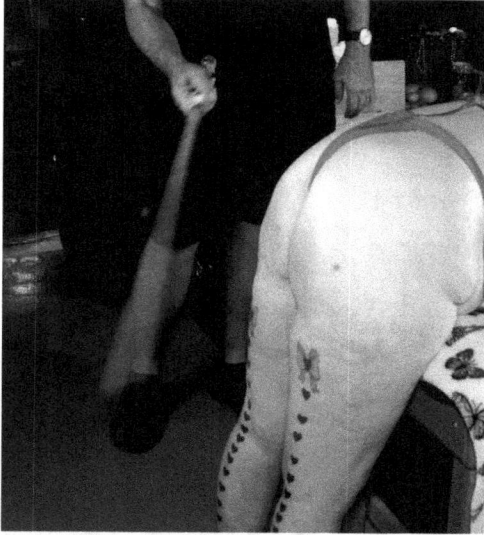

Bent over.

Suspended. If the caning top is not a rigger or familiar with suspension techniques, then this position might require co-topping with someone who is. But suspension provides a different dynamic to cane play. The bottom hangs in various positions, like a piece of meat. Everyone knows their meat is tastier when it is tenderized! The cane is the perfect tool to leave your caning bottom feeling tender.

While these positions are not all-inclusive and the equipment mentioned is not comprehensive, canes are so versatile that it is not a stretch to say that canes can be incorporated into every possible position and type of dungeon equipment imaginable.

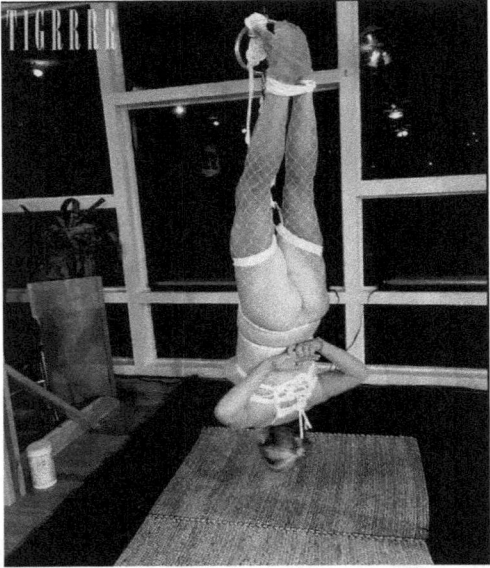

Suspended.

Chapter 12
British vs German Style Caning

MANY STYLES OF caning have evolved worldwide. Two of the most recognizable and teachable styles of caning are the British and German styles. These styles are quite different, and regarding those differences, each caning top will develop their own technique preferences.

German-style caning. This style results in very precise and accurate strikes. Think of the form as very rigid. The arm is locked in place to the side, elbow tucked in, and the swing or strike is done with the forearm, with the wrist locked in place.

A great way to practice this position is to place a sponge in the armpit. Hold the sponge in place with your upper arm. This will lock the arm at the side. The elbow should be bent at a 90-degree angle. Initially, when learning this style, keep the wrist locked as well so the entire stroke is executed with the forearm swing. With the elbow locked at the side, the radius between the elbow and the strike zone is a constant distance, and the accurate finish of the cane is assured.

German style caning does not lend itself to all positions and types of dungeon equipment, but in my opinion accuracy is more easily attained by this style than with using other styles of caning. The style produces horizontal or vertical strokes easily, and any piece of equipment or positioning the cane bottom so that horizontal or vertical strikes can be made will work with this style of caning.

The cane top can adjust their position and angle of the body to reorient the strike so that relative to the cane top the strike is in a horizontal plane or a vertical plane relative to the position of the cane bottom.

Due to the accuracy of German-style caning, it is an exceptional style to pair with bastinado. Bastinado, or precision striking of the feet, must be done accurately and with great control to achieve optimal benefits without inadvertently damaging the feet. I primarily use German-style caning, along with two-cane techniques, when working on the feet or other sensitive areas of the body.

British style caning. British-style caning is more difficult to describe than German-style caning.

Put on your pretend caps and pretend you are a mischievous school student who was called down to the principal's office. The principal bent you over the desk and gave you a punishment caning. They raised their arm above shoulder height with a cane in hand and swung the cane down in an arc, connecting with your bum. The arc of the cane from above the head to its connection with the arse travels in a J or C shape.

The arm is not locked in place, unlike German-style caning. Because the arm is not locked in place, accuracy can be an issue. Sometimes the strike may not end exactly where the top intended, but as long as it is in the vicinity and strikes meaty flesh, no unintentional damage is inflicted.

This style is fun and showier than German-style caning, but it is more challenging and requires a bit of practice to achieve accuracy. However, for precision strikes, German-style caning is much easier to learn and is more accurate right out of the gate.

Six of the Best. In the British school system six of the best was a classic punishment given where 5 strokes formed ladders evenly spaced at 1" apart and the sixth stroke formed a diagonal angled across the first 5 strokes from one butt cheek to the other. Male students historically received cane strokes while female students were stuck with birch bundles.

British style caning.

Chapter 13

Free-form Caning with Gloryus

THIS CHAPTER WILL share how I found free-form caning and why it continues to develop my play through interactive music, feedback, and the incorporation of energy.[7]

My name is Gloryus. I have been free-form caning from the beginning of my journey with rattan canes, circa 2009. I had the good fortune to experience canes in scenes at my home dungeon, APEX, with different skilled tops, mentors, guides, and bottoms who, I had learned, have a wealth of experience and knowledge.

At that time, we also had several well-known out-of-state presenters who would come and do classes for us. Catherine Gross was the first person that I saw using a 36-inch cane. MsBonnie of the Dragon Clan, who continues to be one of my mentors to this day, also used and uses longer canes. I had no idea they came in that length, as I had not yet started creating canes for myself through my shop, Calamity Canes! This has since been rectified and the travesty corrected. I have added several 36" canes to my own collection, as well as make them to sell at local events. The

---

7 My dear friend and leather sister, Gloryus from Phoenix was kind enough to write this chapter describing her connection to caning and her somewhat unique caning style.

different techniques for using the longer canes were developed during my primal play, and the evolution of my free-form style added another nuance to the growing list of skills.

The Whiplash technique, which Dex introduced in Chapter 7, was just me trying to reach the other side of my bottom faster than I was physically able to. The Whiplash Stroke was a huge aha moment, opening up multiple possibilities, and has since developed into a unique life of its own, with variations in speed, ramping, and delivery intensity. It can be a scene on its own and take the bottom on a journey. When I first bounced that cane, near the handle, and struck the butt cheek! OMGoodness!

Seeing my bottom's head spin around fast enough to cause a whiplash brought me so much joy! I really hoped they would add this moment to their feedback, and if not, I was prepared to ask for it.

I then started adding speed to the strikes. Being able to send the tip of the cane onto the back, with what seemed like quadrupled Force – became a new rush! That the cane seemed to lay across the back's entirety was a huge turn on. The bolster, which I place under the upper thigh area to lift the buttocks up and protect the kidneys, was all the encouragement that was needed to continue exploring, with the bottom's permission of course.

Free-form tipping and the Whiplash work well together and can be easily incorporated as I walk around the table and pass near the feet. I point the tip of the cane in the direction of the bottom's head. I bounce the cane on each cheek, with the target area landing onto each shoulder blade. This is the focus strike zone.

The Whiplash can also be done in the opposite direction, per my evolution. I found that standing near their head, bouncing off their shoulder near the handle, and allowing the tip of the cane to strike the butt cheek before continuing my journey around the table, was very fluid. While circling I continued tipping upper arms, butt cheeks, shoulders, calves, back up to butt cheeks, whiplash, and so on. The bottom can lose direction and not know where I'm standing. This is a small nuance to the scene but builds our trust journey.

Whiplash cane at its finish
during Gloryus' scene.

The English laying of strikes techniques, tipping, and whiplash are all currently in my repertoire. They've been a driving force behind my free-form caning style, and I don't see that changing. I am looking forward to seeing how it continues to evolve in my play.

In my journey, I learned that canes definitely did, do, and can hurt. To me, it felt like they were going from zero to 100 straight out of the gate. At the beginning of my journey, I didn't understand the importance of breathing and allowing the vibrations to go through me. While I know this is not an accurate interpretation of the actual events or intentions of those who sought to mentor me, it did leave me in a leery headspace to continue trying canes at all from the bottom side.

Then, I met Dex at Thunder in the Mountains, where we had negotiated a whip scene online for the first dungeon night. As you may have already guessed, it was amazing! He is definitely skilled in his craft, and he seemed to enjoy throwing his whips at me! Our scene went better than I could have hoped for, and we agreed to play again!

On the second Dungeon play night, he asked if I wanted to try canes. I hesitantly agreed after he showed me what was in his case, and I got to meet "the Girls" for the first time. My thoughts rushed at me! Like... someone who has mermaids on his canes has to have some whimsical yet sadistic tendencies! Right? The Girls were a beautiful collection of rattan canes in different thicknesses and lengths! So here was Dex asking me to try canes, in a humongous ballroom dungeon at Thunder in the Mountains, lying on my tummy in front of a hundred some people, naked, and I was still unsure about the weapon of choice. I still didn't feel that I would be able to embrace the pain as I had witnessed other bottoms do.

Not only was I incorrect, but Dex, how he played, sent me down a new path altogether. It was the first time that playfulness accompanied the strikes. This was the beginning of my love affair with canes and my journey into demystifying cane strokes for others.

I am a very primal player and can lose myself to the energy between myself and the bottom. I enjoy the guiding aspect of topping and it is the icing on the cake. I can feel music to my core, its throbbing bass, the rests, the crescendo! What I found when I topped and let go was that the cane was bouncing in my hands and in time to the music! I had stopped holding back and found that I could dance and drop energy all over: non-traditionally (not English) and free flowing.

It felt like I was holding, instead of a cane, a magical wand and dropping energy balls into all of the places that I touched while Tipping. Learning the different vibrations that carried my energy through the cane and into the bottom was now a new game. The frequencies of my play partners' moans, the way their bodies relaxed, the acceptance of a harder strike, and so much more, adding to the nuances of an ever-evolving dance – it all filled me with newfound energy and an excitement that drew bottoms to my table.

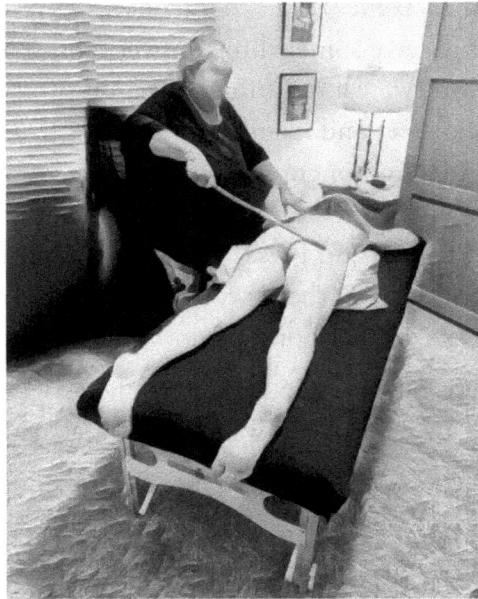

Gloryus tipping, a slightly different technique using the last 4" of the cane.

Giving the dance its lead and trying to note the differences while staying in the moment became difficult, but it was totally worth it. If I found myself doing the same movements over and over, I gave that movement a name. Yes! I totally understand that everything I do has probably been done before, and it's even, in this very moment, being recreated again in another kinkster's journey, and of course, being shared by Dex through this book.

Education on all things caning, even to this day, remains fresh and inspires me to experiment as I grow my craft. I needed feedback and wanted to share this invigorating style of play with others.

The bottom's feedback after a scene, in my personal opinion, is vital for this growth. I have literally changed some of how I play based on shared feedback. My negotiations include that they send me a written response after 3 days that addresses "What they liked, what they did not care for, and what they never have to experience again and why."

With permission, here is some of the feedback I received from one of my cane bottoms. The takeaway for me here was that giving them wiggle room (I wiggle the cane as a reminder to relax completely and exhale the breath they just took in) before striking sternly was definitely the way to go!

~Joy after the Primal Party feedback:

"I loved experiencing canes with you the other night. You made the experience magical. I have never experienced anything like that before. You made everything flow, and you took me on a journey to a faraway place. I did not know anything was happening around us. You captivated me, holding my mind and energy the whole time. I didn't have to think about anything because I knew you were keeping me safe and taking care of me.

I love how you coached me through the whole experience. You let me know what you were going to do beforehand and the cues you were going to give me to breathe, and you reminded me of this throughout the entire experience.

The music you selected set the mood and kept me in tune

with you. I have never experienced music as part of the scene, and I see now that it can change the whole atmosphere.

I enjoyed that you started lighter and built the intensity as you continued on. I love that you progressively upped the intensity throughout the scene and helped to push my limits gradually. You took me to a safe place that allowed me to relax and enjoy what was being given to me.

I am so thankful for you and this experience. I have been in the best mood since. You put my mind and body in a place of peace and comfort. I am so thankful for this experience with you and I look forward to a time when we can do this again. Thank you so much!!"

We have played several times since, and neither of us has expressed disappointment to the other. Her feedback at the end of our three-day respite and decompression from the scene also became part of our negotiation for the next time we convene our play.

I implement free-form caning using a stroke I call Tipping. I use the bottom two to three inches of the cane and create a vortex around the bottom, who is lying on the table. This is done in time to the music, and with each heavy beat, I make sure that the tip of that cane is landing on a meaty part of their body.

Walking around the table gives the bottom a feeling of anticipation, as they don't know where the hits are coming from, and this can become a very light-hearted interaction with laughter which starts us on the road to trust. It also creates a very meditative state. That, along with the development of trust, is what I feel makes it easier for them to receive harder strokes later.

Breathing is everything! When negotiating, I will introduce a form of guided meditation for us to practice in the scene. I share verbal instructions with the bottom on how to use breathing during play to move energy.

For example: a visualization that, as they take a breath in, the air flows through the inside of their body, pulling up any negative energy. It will then be released with their breath and into a cloud. I ask the bottom to visualize that any darkness within will begin to fill a white cloud that is in front of them. As the cloud gets darker and heavier, it will fall, and with their next big breath, they can draw in another pristine cloud to fill.

This not only promotes relaxation but speeds up our connection as we are doing this together. When I strike and lay a line, they know that on my end, the strike is not to be held, that I am cutting through the energy and pushing it through them, through the table, through the floor, and away from us.

Free-form caning isn't just about moving around the table, dancing, and pushing energy; we are creating a vortex for the bottom and I. It is the inclusion of trust developed by tapping the tip of the cane all over the body to create a methodical massage-like sensation that grants us space to explore.

It does not mean that I'm not going to lay down cane strokes across their buttocks and their thighs, but it is the way that we are able to do so more readily. Trust has been developed, and they are able to say yes and receive.

What I've shared is from my own personal journey. It is ever evolving, and I am ever changing. I am ever-growing, developing additional nuances to add to my cane crafting. But what do I know? - I am just a girl with a stick.

Gloryus [8]

---

[8] Watching Gloryus free-form cane is like watching a magician with a wand, an energy wand doing magick on the lucky bottom who's receiving her energy. Connected with the music and the chakras, it is a wonderful sight to behold.

Chapter 14
Marking

THE CANE IS one of the easiest implements to use for marking. Cane marks create a pallet that inspire kinky photography.

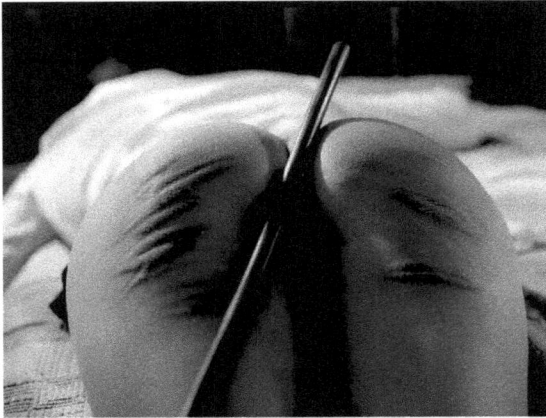

Artistic marks.

During negotiations, ensure that the cane bottom is okay with marks. I personally do not guarantee any cane bottom that there will not be any marks. There are too many variables in whether someone will mark or not.

Skin tone, genetics, age, whether someone tans, and complexion, along with other variables, all play a role in whether someone will mark. An impact bottom who is played with regularly may develop what is known as a leather butt or back. Their skin will actually transform when played with, becoming resistant to strikes. It will take on a leather-like texture. This type of skin will develop ridges in form when caned, and often, even though ridges are present, it will be resistant to marking.

Many cane bottoms actually want marks. They wear them like badges to be shown off. They also play a part in self-aftercare. The day or week after a scene, a cane bottom can look in a mirror and see their marks, recalling the feelings and emotions of the caning scene.

Some generalizations can be made about canes and marks. Thick canes can cause deep tissue damage, essentially bruising the skin and muscle tissue. Thin canes leave a clean line and a mark drawn on the skin by the cane strike. These lines, when caning precisely, can create patterns. This is most often a scene with thin cane strikes forming a ladder down the butt and back of the thighs.

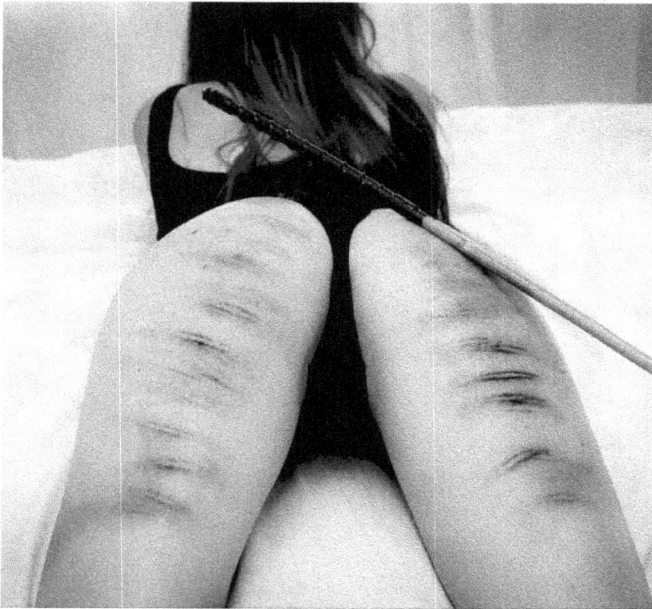

Ladders.

Another generalization is that with a good warmup, partial strokes using almost any technique can be done, and for most cane bottoms, the day after, there will be very few marks remaining, if any at all. The butt will be able to display a nice, even red.

The opposite generalization is also true. Without a warm-up, what is sometimes called cold caning, marks are assured, even when using only partial strokes. Warm-up is that important. Cold caning is often used in a punishment caning setting. However, cold caning can be a negotiated approach to a scene when the cane bottom insists on marks.

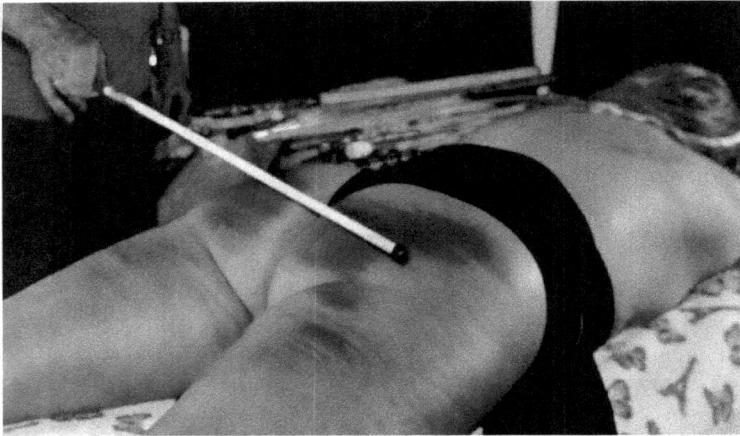

Evenly red.

Treating marks can be part of the aftercare process. Soothing lotions can be applied to the caned area. Arnica cream can help shorten the healing time and minimize bruising. If the skin is broken, an antibiotic ointment can be applied to the affected area.

Chapter 15
Corporal Punishment and Discipline

CORPORAL PUNISHMENT HAS historically been applied in three societal contexts: judicial, parental, and school corporal punishment.

Judicial corporal punishment is the infliction of punishment as a result of a sentence imposed on an offender by a court judgment. Traditional punishments included flogging or whipping, strapping, birching,[9] caning, bastinado, or falaka. Judicial corporal punishment is still practiced in some countries.

Parental corporal punishment is any act causing deliberate physical pain or discomfort to a child in response to some undesired behavior. Historically, it involved spanking or paddling with an open hand or an implement such as a paddle or a belt in an attempt at behavior modification.

Corporal punishment in schools is the deliberate infliction of physical pain as a response to undesired behavior by students. In schools, the teacher or principal administering the punishment would typically strike the student on the butt or the palms of the

---

9 Birching is a form of corporal punishment with a birch rod. A birch rod is not a single rod and historically was made from birch twigs, but in modern times it can also be made from any strong and smooth branches of trees or shrubs, such as willow tied into a tight bundle..

hands with an implement. Traditional implements included a rattan cane, a birch rod, a paddle, a tawse, and a leather belt or strap.

Corporal punishment in school in the English-speaking world originated in the British practice of the 19th and 20th centuries, particularly in boys' schools, where teenage boys were disciplined with rattan punishment canes. The use of corporal punishment in schools has been justified by the common-law doctrine of *in loco parentis*, which grants authority figures in schools the same rights as parents to discipline and punish children for not following school rules. Some Asian countries also follow this practice.

Singapore has a long history of caning as a punishment used in a wide variety of contexts: judicial, prison, reformatory, military, school, and domestic. A Singapore cane is 1.2 meters long and 12 mm in diameter restricted to a maximum of 24 strokes and limited in application to males under 50 y.o.

Role Play. The historical applications of all three types of corporal punishment provide a perfect backdrop for role-play. To be clear, role-play described here is only between consenting adults.

Examples include the dressed-up police officer bringing the suspect before the judge to be tried in a mock trial and punished on the corporal punishment theme night of a play party. Or the scene could be relationship-oriented, with the Daddy or Mommy figure interacting with their "little," who is in a submissive role. Corporal punishment sets a perfect stage for the cane to take center stage as an implement.

At the end of summer, back-to-school BDSM play parties are THE thing in the scene. This is the perfect time for tops to dress up as schoolmarms or headmasters, and for the bottoms to dress up in little sexy student outfits. Mock classrooms with fun rules to be broken lead into settings where some naughty students are called to the front of the room to have their pants pulled down and be caned in front of the entire class. How humiliatingly fun?

If a harsher scene is negotiated, the top can use techniques from the corporal punishment style of caning, such as no warm-up, cold caning, and ensuring the caning hurts and produces the desired endorphin rush. One aspect of corporal punishment is to eliminate all pauses and breathing room between strikes. This prevents the bottom from fully processing the strike before the next strike hits.

Classic teacher/student role-play: School teacher caning naughty student.

Chapter 16

Pain Management

ONE MIGHT NOT consider pain management as part of a great cane scene, but it is. There are several aspects to consider when managing pain during a scene. The participants on both ends of the cane are involved.

Breathing. Breathing is an essential part of energy exchange. The body breathes life in, and energy enters the body. It exhales, releasing tension, excess energy, and contaminants. Holding your breath traps all those things inside your body. The cane bottom must breathe before a heavy strike. A savvy cane top, like Gloryus, will tell or use an agreed upon signal, to let the bottom know they should breathe right before they are going to deliver a heavy strike. The top can also provide verbal or non-verbal guidance for the bottom to exhale and continue breathing after a heavy strike or multiple strikes. This is part of the process of removing excess energy and settling into the caning.

Reading Body Language. When a cane bottom needs time to breathe and process energy, the body language often gives it away. A cane top who is paying attention will pause and let the cane bottom breathe. They will allow the pain to travel through the body and dissipate. When the body language reflects calm energy, the session can resume.

Mixed methods or techniques. When a series of cane strikes creates a pain burst, another pain management strategy is to mix the methods or techniques being used, as well as the type of cane. Switching from a thin cane that has caused a pain burst to a thicker one is one method. Changing the technique from, say, a strike-through with a thin cane to bouncing with a thick cane will help disperse the energy.

Distractions. Introducing a distraction can also be a pain management strategy. If one area of the body, say, the buttocks, is being used for a ramping-up technique, switch it up a bit. At the peak of the strikes, instead of allowing the body to process the pain and creating a pause, shift the strikes to a different part of the body. When moving to a different target area, the top may also vary the technique. This will distract the bottom from the pain they are still processing.

Rubbing. Rubbing the strike area, light scratching, or gently touching the fingers on the bottom's strike area can aid in pain management. Human touch can be soothing, comforting, and reassuring. In the case of a cane scene, it may also be the prelude for more pain.

Erotic touch. Certainly, erotic touch must be negotiated clearly before a scene starts, and what is allowed and what is not is clearly consented to by the bottom. But erotic touch and massage are definitely a pain management strategy. In fact, mixing pain and pleasure is one of the hallmarks of BDSM. It is what attracts many to kink in the first place. Many people into BDSM do not like vanilla sex. It is about rough consensual play, and yes, erotic touch sometimes culminating in sex between consenting adults.

Chapter 17

Occasions for Caning

THERE ARE MANY occasions for a caning scene, especially for the caning enthusiast. But here is a list of occasions that you can build off of and add your own occasions to make this chapter your own.

1. A negotiated caning scene.
2. A birthday caning.
3. A relationship maintenance caning.
4. A punishment caning.
5. A caning is incorporated into a game. (Ex. Tic-Tac-Toe)
6. A caning by the teacher.
7. A caning by the principal.
8. A caning by the priest or nun.
9. A co-topping cane scene.
10. A co-bottoming cane scene.
11. A 4th of July caning.
12. A Happy New Year's caning.
13. A caning for marks.
14. A caning for massage.
15. A caning/bastinado for the feet.
16. Bastinado to increase the circulation in the feet of a diabetic.
17. Bastinado to improve plantar fasciitis

18. A caning for an endorphin rush.
19. A mixed implement scene incorporating a cane.
20. _____
21. _____
22. _____
23. _____
24. _____
25. _____

Chapter 18
Energizing the Chakras and Dark Energy

THERE ARE FEW SM implements that deliver the energy level of a bullwhip. A rattan cane is one of those implements. The selling point of rattan canes is that while a bullwhip requires excellent eye-hand coordination and hours of practice to safely throw in a dimly lit dungeon, a rattan cane can be wielded efficiently by every top. It is an energy stick that can be used for light, feathered strokes all the way up to intense, focused strokes. The energy passes from the top to the bottom through the cane.

What does this energy do when it enters the body? Where does it go? How does it travel? What responses does it produce? Some of this is known. When a cane strikes a bundle of nerves, such as in the foot with bastinado, that energy is translated into electric impulses that travel through the nervous system and trigger responses in other parts of the body. It is known that the energy of a cane strike triggers a chemical response in the body, and the brain releases endorphins. That pain translates into pleasure at some locations.

Energizing the chakras. The ancient system of chakras is a helpful way to visualize the flow of energy through the body. When a chakra is open, it allows energy to flow. When it is closed, it stops, restricts, or limits the transfer of energy.

A great way to begin a cane scene is to work with the chakras during warm-up. Using a bass or baritone cane, begin with gentle tapping or bouncing on the heart chakra (across the shoulder blades). Use partial strokes and listen and feel the energy flowing into the heart chakra. As it enters the chest cavity, it will resonate and send sound waves through the chakra. This energy in the chest cavity will remind you of thumping a watermelon to see if it is ripe.

Once the heart chakra is warmed up, include the root chakra using similar techniques. Not only are you warming up a primary cane strike area, but you are energizing the root chakra. With light bouncing with partial strokes, move up and down the back between the shoulders and the butt. Avoid hitting the tailbone. The goal is to encourage and stimulate the flow of energy between the heart and root chakras throughout the entire chakra system.

Add the back of the legs to this pattern of light partial tapping, avoiding the back of the knees and the Achilles tendon area. Focus on the meaty part of the back of the legs. Add light taps to the middle of the heels. Watch and feel energy entering the feet and traveling up the legs to the root chakra. Bastinado will be discussed in a future chapter. I do not consider this to be Bastinado. It is just including part of the feet in the warmup routine and encouraging energy flow up and down the chakra system.

Once heavier cane play is started on the root chakra, the sweet spot,[10] and the back of the hamstrings, do not neglect the heart chakra. Use partial strokes on the heart chakra. Open the chest cavity to energy and encourage it to travel down to the root chakra by following the energy path with partial strokes down the back.

Always protect the tailbone with the off hand, or by skipping

---

10 Sweet spot: the area or crease between the bottom of the butt and the top of the back of the thigh. A well-placed stroke will resonate energy in the genital area, regardless of whether the individual is male or female.

over it. Add a heavier stroke to the root chakra and continue down the legs with partial strokes, avoiding the back of the knees and the Achilles' tendon. Then, end with a stroke on the middle of the heel, at the bottom of both feet. This will encourage energy to flow from its entry point in the foot, up the legs, to the root chakra, and through the chakras to the heart chakra.

Engage the throat chakra by asking the bottom questions and encouraging sound (mmms, ahhs, ohhhh, owws) from the throat chakra. This not only provides feedback but also activates feedback from the crown chakra, triggering subsequent chemical activity in the crown chakra, which can be verbalized, even if it isn't spoken. Sounds are beneficial and add vibration and energy flow.

Not all bottoms are expressive during a cane scene. Still, during negotiations, the top can discuss with the bottom that verbal sounds are encouraged and helpful —not only for the top in reading body language, but also as a way to energize the throat chakra. Bottoms that become non-verbal and recognize that their throat chakra is closing can try to make sounds that do not require verbalization, such as slapping the table or the cross.

Dark energy. I was at a planetarium when someone asked the astronomer giving the presentation to explain dark energy in the universe. He said it is particles of energy traveling along an ever-expanding, widening path across the universe. He used the analogy of a balloon and said that if a Sharpie were used to put evenly spaced black dots on an uninflated balloon, when the balloon was blown up, the dots would gradually become farther apart as the balloon expanded. They would travel on an ever-expanding path as more air was blown into the balloon.

So the description of dark energy on the somatic level from a cane strike is that energy enters the body at a specific, very precise point from the cane. It travels in ever-expanding waves through the soma.

Some bottoms describe this level of intense cane strike, which produces dark energy on the somatic level, as a starburst. This, too, is a similar analogy. As a star bursts or explodes, it travels in all directions in an ever-expanding path from the point of explosion. Sometimes this starburst appears in the crown chakra as endorphins explode into action.

The direction of energy travel is not always in every direction. It depends upon where the cane strike is. A cane strike that enters the bottom of the feet travels in one direction because of anatomy. Sure, it travels around the foot, but the nerve endings in the bottom of the feet focus the energy up the leg. A cane strike on the palm will likewise travel primarily up the arm, where a cane strike on the butt will travel omnidirectionally.

Dark energy on the somatic level has not been scientifically proven. It is a common-sense analogy to help understand the intense energy that a cane transmits to the bottom.

Chapter 19

Bastinado

BASTINADO IS THE precise striking of the foot with a cane or rod. Bastinado originated as a punishment, but the BDSM application is focused on pain and pleasure and energy transfer through the bottom of the feet. Feet in bastinado should be viewed individually, with the characteristics of each foot, both left and right, to be explored.

What it is not is falaka. Falaka is a discipline or punishment ritual that involves binding the ankles or feet together and striking the feet in punishment. In falaka, both feet are hit simultaneously. It often results in broken bones in the feet. It is associated with Middle Eastern cultures.

Great bastinado is based on the idea that each foot is different and will respond similarly, but differently when treated separately. Bastinado, in the context and paradigm of BDSM and dungeon play, involves yet another form of energy play, only this time the focus is on the foot.

Foot chart. The feet are the foundation of the body. They are full of nerve endings that connect to the nervous system and extend to various extremities, internal organs, and components of the somatic system. Google a diagram of foot massage, and you will see this system illustrated. Most foot charts come with a disclaimer that everyone's feet are different and that there will be differences even between the right and left feet of each person.

While looking at a foot diagram is helpful to a top or someone interested in bastinado or even foot massage, it is not a set-in-stone diagram. It provides valuable information and a solid foundation for understanding the feet and their interconnection with the rest of the body.

Bastinado is excellent therapy for the feet. It can almost feel like a foot massage. It increases the circulation in the feet. It warms up the feet. It is like physical therapy when used to aid and treat foot ailments, such as tight arches and plantar fasciitis. It is excellent for diabetics, as it aids circulation and nerve stimulation in the feet.

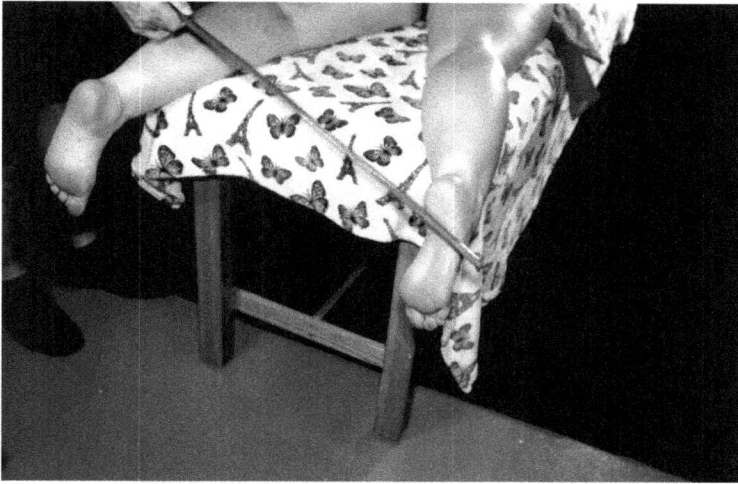

Bastinado. Heel/arch partial stroke.

Self-bastinado. How hard can you strike the feet? This is a common question, often asked at bastinado workshops. This is where self-bastinado is very important. Begin by using a raw rattan short cane, a shortie, about 18" long. Raw rattan has not been conditioned and is less dense. There is less chance of damaging the feet when learning just how hard you can hit them. This is why you are learning on your own feet.

Explore your own feet. Learn what feels good and what does not.

See how hard you can hit your own feet, without damaging them, and note when it becomes too much. By striking your own foot, you get a real good idea of how to warm up the feet, how hard you can hit, and where the best strike zones are. Bastinado is about precise foot strikes, and accuracy is essential.

You might even find that you like a little bastinado after a long day on your feet at work.

Partial strokes. Almost every technique taught in Chapter 7 can be brought over and applied to bastinado. The only technique not recommended is strike-through. Bouncing is especially effective. Partial strokes aid in accuracy. If you feel you are not accurate enough to have confidence in using a 30" cane for bastinado, then use a shorter 24" cane. Still not confident? Then use a shortie (18" cane).

Two-cane technique. Many people still feel like they are not accurate enough with their cane strikes to do a bastinado scene. Malarky! Use a two-cane technique.

In the dominant hand, hold the striking cane. In the non-dominant hand, have the anchor cane or guide rod cane. Anchor the guide rod cane adjacent to the precise strike zone on the foot, then, using the strike cane, slide the cane down the guide rod to finish a partial stroke exactly where it should be placed. Success! Everyone can do bastinado.

Preparing the foot for bastinado. I recommend rubbing massage oil on the feet before bastinado. I like a light oil. Some people are allergic to peanut oil, but almond or sesame oil is lighter and can be used to prepare the feet for bastinado. This human touch is nice, and many bottoms like having their feet touched and rubbed. A good foot rub is a nice beginning.

Some people have very sensitive feet and cannot tolerate their feet being touched. If this is the case, do not rub oil on their feet. Another technique will be described later in the chapter.

Warmup. A good warm-up is essential for bastinado, just as it is for a good cane scene. Bringing the skin up to temperature prepares the feet for more moderately intense bastinado strikes.

For bottoms with sensitive feet, begin warmup by ignoring the feet. Begin warmup with the root chakra. After a couple of minutes, lightly strike one of the feet, immediately returning warmup to the butt. Increase the occurrence of occasional foot strikes during warmup and diminish the number of strikes on the butt. Eventually the feet will be warmed up and the sensitivity will be gone replaced with trust and comfort with the cane strikes.

Exploration. Exploring and reading body language is key to great bastinado. The foot chart only gives an idea of where interesting strike zones might be on the foot. The best foot chart is one created during the warmup by closely watching the bottom's response to strikes on different parts of the feet.

Verbal feedback is a direct way to gain knowledge of a particular bottom's feet. Realize the left foot will not be the same as the right foot. Treat them individually. I rec-ommend not striking both feet at once, as you will want to read each foot individually.

Bastinado is often not an exciting scene. It is a quiet scene between top and bottom, like a spa day —it feels so good. It can be a way to reward a great bottom and give them something back for the service they have provided to a Dom or top.

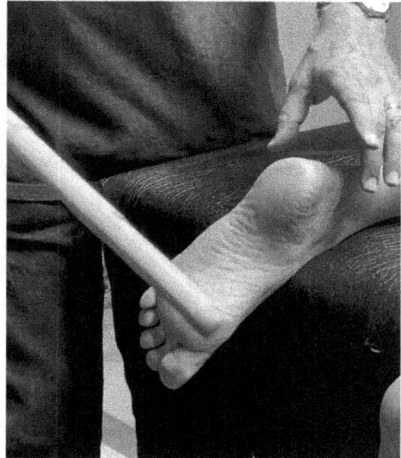

Metatarsal bastinado.

Reading body language. This is the key to great bastinado, as everyone's foot is different. Everyone's sweet spot on the feet will be in a slightly different location. Not everyone will even have a sweet spot on their foot, but when someone does, that sweet spot can be played with and manipulated, in building the bottom to orgasm from a foot strike.

Energy travels from the sweet spot up the legs to the root chakra, energizing it. Sometimes, this energy encourages an erotic response from the bottom. Most often this results in a slight rise of the buttocks and sometimes a moan from the bottom.

When exploring the feet, pay attention to the energy traveling up the legs to the root chakra. Take note of locations where that resonance appears to be the best and where the butt responds to a foot strike. Aha, I found it. So do not let on that you found it, but continue to strike and move strikes around. Yet note every time you hit the sweet spot, you gain a response from the root chakra.

Build these responses, climb them up the ladder to the edge, and encourage them to go over the edge into orgasm. Once an orgasm has been teased and coaxed on one foot, shift to the other foot and see if you can find its sweet spot. Repeat this process on the other foot and see if a second orgasm comes easier.

Some individuals are multi-orgasmic, while others are not. Some individuals may not have a sweet spot, or if they do, they may not feel comfortable expressing it in public play. Everyone is unique, and no two feet are the same. This is one reason bastinado, as with caning, never gets boring.

Tuning Your Cane

TUNING YOUR CANE primarily applies to rattan canes. The goal is to achieve optimal resonance, vibration, and energy transfer with the cane. Strike a cane against the heel of your hand. Feel its vibrations and resonance. Feel the energy enter the heel of your hand and travel up your arm. Does the cane feel alive or dead? Try this with several canes in your cane ensemble. If you identify a cane that feels dead, it might just need tuning.

I'll share a true story about the Girls. Some of it was recounted in Chapter 2, but I will repeat it here as the background is needed.

My first canes were a trio of raw rattan canes I bought from Hanson Paddle at the Boston Fetish Flea in 2001. I purchased a thick cane, a slightly thinner one, and a thin one. As I learned more about canes, these two thicker canes (a baritone and a second tenor) became two of my favorite warm-up canes.

When Whyppie made the first generation of mermaid canes, I began exclusively playing with the Girls when I would do a cane scene. It was this first generation of canes that had such an impact (no pun intended) on Gloryus and opened her to a love of canes.

I loved the Girls so much, but honestly, I missed playing with those two Hanson paddle "sticks," as Whyppie refers to them, made of raw rattan. They both had an incredible resonance and were positioned between the deep bass cane in the set of Girls and the alto cane in the ensemble. I felt it was time to expand the girls' line and introduce a second generation of mermaid canes.

So Whyppie went to work. I mailed her the Hanson "sticks" and asked her also to add a whangee cane and a Sanibel beach cane (a rod with sand from the beach epoxied to it).

When I got the second generation of canes back and tested them, I noticed that the transformed Hanson Paddle raw rattan sticks were dead. Adding handles to them had altered the resonance and the frequency of energy transfer, and now these conditioned and finished, beautiful Crown Jewel canes were dead. Conditioning the raw rattan changed the density of the canes, and adding handles also altered their balance. Most importantly, though, these two elements changed the cane's resonance and frequency, and in this case, it dampened it.

Here's how I fixed them and how I suggest tuning your own canes:

I took the canes over to my friend, Octoberman (r.i.p.), and asked him to carefully cut off 1/4" at a time off the tip of these canes. After each cut, I would test the cane against the heel of my hand and check its vibration and resonance. Slow and steady is the way to go, as once you have cut off material, it cannot be added back on. After a few cuts, the canes felt wonderful again, and I had restored the resonance to optimal energy transfer. I sanded the ends of the canes to round off the tips again, and my canes were tuned.

Appendix B

Cane Carrying Cases

This should sound simple, but it simply is not. Carrying canes around a vanilla world without calling attention to the fact that you are leather or interested in BDSM is not as easy as it sounds. Ideally, you want a vanilla-looking case that doesn't draw unnecessary attention to you.

Often, the ideal case is not viable. Rattan actually is a vine and is porous. Depending upon the size and source, a cane maker's first task is to straighten it. But straightened rattan sometimes wants to return to its original shape, or at least regain a slight curve. So not only for carrying from one place to another, but also for storing your canes, ideally, you want to keep them straight.

Length is also another consideration. Most canes are 24-30" in length. I prefer 30" canes, but many of my friends swear by the 24" ones. An 18" shortie and even a 24" cane will easily fit in most toy bags. 30" and 36" canes are not so easy to find cases for.

The very best cane case, unfortunately, is an automatic rifle case. It has foam, which can be slotted to fit your canes and keep them straight. I'm sure you don't want to be carrying an automatic rifle case into a hotel, convention center, or even into a private home for a BDSM event or play party. It violates public rules of conduct and draws undue attention to yourself.

Two decades ago, I settled on an arrow case designed for competitive bow shooting. This case was long enough for 30" canes (but not 36" ones), and it had foam inside with little slots that held the canes completely straight. It worked perfectly for thinner canes. For the thicker ones, the foam had to be trimmed.

This worked for many years, carrying the Girls. At some point, the foam rubber began to deteriorate, leaving a residue on the canes. I had to refurbish the case. I went to a craft store and bought a sheet of high-density foam, glued it in place, and cut custom-sized slots for the Girls. This second edition of the case was actually better than the original because all the slots were cut explicitly for the Girls.

Over the years, while traveling and doing cane workshops, folks would give me a cane or rod — or even a set of canes or rods — as a present. My orchestra grew to the point that I needed a new case. I had a canvas bag with a draw string that worked for a while, but soon my collection of pervertibles required expansion.

We live in Florida, a land of many golfers, and one interesting thing about golfers is that every few years, they seem to think they need a new golf bag. One day, when we were driving the dog around on a golf cart, the light bulb went off in my head. A golf bag was the perfect cane case, especially for rods and pervertibles. I picked up the "free" bag at the curb and took it home.

The full-size golf bag literally swallowed my cane, and I had to go fishing just to pull a cane out. It was too deep, but it gave me an idea. What about a youth bag? I searched Amazon, and I discovered that there are actually golf bags made for 3-6 year olds. These are perfect! And most of them come with a tripod and a cover. So literally, you look like an adult or grandparent carrying your kid's golf bag. You walk into the play space, pop the tripod, unzip the cover, and bam, you are ready to play. All of your canes are organized in the wood and iron slots.

Appendix C
Resources and Cane Vendors

THE BEST SOURCE for info on a spectrum of techniques and dungeon play with canes is this book. Thank you for purchasing it. The set of supplementary instructional videos for caning and also bastinado can be found at *http://witd.houseofgraves.com*

Of course my YouTube channel, The Leather Journey, also has most of these videos in the Caning and Bastinado playlists. Thank you for your free subscription.

There are a couple of excellent essays and shorter works on caning that I can recommend. Check them out online [Hawks, n.d.; Hugs (2004)]. Full citation is in the References.

Sourcing.[11] As I travel around the country, I find someone making and vending canes in almost every region. I encourage everyone to check out the cane vendors in their area.

---

11 There are 13 generas and over 600 species of rattan. Most of the trade names are associated with a single variety of rattan that is linked to their source of origin, i.e. Manau, Malacca, Semambu, Tohiti, and Manila. Dragon and Kooboo are trade names not associated with a single species or single variety of rattan, but are rather trade name descriptors for characteristics found in canes. Kooboo are flexible, lighter grade, and more plentiful in source. Dragon is a premium trade name that is denser and has nodes farther apart. Manau and Malacca are single variety and source of origin premium trade names.

Gloryus at Calamity Canes offers rattan canes with incredible energy. A large part of that is due to the positive energy of the person who is making the canes. You can contact her on Fetlife to inquire.

However, if you have a personal fetish for buying a rattan cane from someone who can turn it into a work of art, then there is no one other than Whyppie at Canes4Pain. *http://canes4pain.com*

Of course, Whyppie offers a variety of canes, ranging from those with colorful handles to BDSM fine art, in all price ranges.

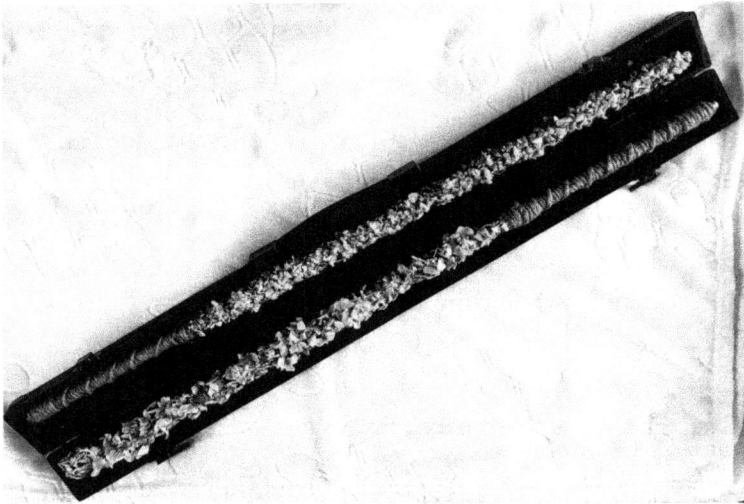

Canes4Pain shelly canes. What a master cane maker does after a day at the beach.

I recently began making my own line of canes. In an act of shameless self-promotion, I suggest you check out Exotic Hardwood Canes by Dex. You can purchase them in my Etsy shop or contact me on Fetlife for better pricing (no middleman) and the same quality cane.

Tops, Bottoms and Canes

Safety is a two-way street and a crucial part of negotiations for a cane scene for both the top and bottom. There are several aspects to safety.

Cleanliness is cane godliness. The canes used in your scene must be clean.

If the cane is porous and has come into contact with bodily fluids or blood, it ideally should not be used on another cane bottom. However, if it has been cleaned with due diligence using a hospital-grade cold sterilant antiviral/antibacterial cleaner and then cleaned with alcohol, and both parties are in agreement, it can be used under the RACK play protocols.

In pickup play, cane bottoms should not rely on an unfamiliar top to clean the canes. They should offer, and almost insist, for their own peace of mind, to clean the canes that are going to be used on them before they play. In many instances, the best approach to safe caning for the heavy cane bottom is for the bottom to own their own canes that are only used on them.

Location, Location, Location. Yes, this is exactly like a real estate deal. Do not strike the back of the knees, any tendon or cartilage areas of the body, or bones. Avoid the tailbone area. Strike thick, meaty areas of the body. The primary safe area for heavy strikes is the buttocks - otherwise known as the bottom's ass. Other areas that are only partially meaty require common sense and keeping the strike to a gentle, partial stroke (such as the upper arms and calves).

Health Concerns and Medications.

Be informed of any health issues in the pre-scene negotiations.

I do not espouse heavy cane strikes on someone who's on blood thinners of any type. That does not mean a cane scene cannot be successful if the bottom is on blood thinners. The cane is a magickal energy stick. There is a broad spectrum of partial strokes that can be done with a slow energy build-up without leaving lasting marks or breaking blood vessels.

Consent goes both ways. As a loving dominant, and conscientious top, I would not consent to heavy play or do a cane scene with someone on blood thinners who was expecting heavy marks and bruises. On the other end of that stick (haha), the bottom has an obligation to inform the top of all medications that might be important in an impact scene, such as caning.

Caning Bottom's Mantra. "I will not be caned by any top that I have not seen wield a cane." Cane play, by definition, is edge play. It is not like bottoming for a hand spanking or flogging. While a cane can produce a wide range of sensations and produce energy exchanges on a spectrum, it can take someone quickly to the edge of their endorphin cliff.

Know what you are getting into with a top when you negotiate a cane scene. Remember, it took me two days to negotiate a cane scene with Gloryus all those years ago. But the result was worth every minute of effort as it was a scene I will never forget. May all of your cane scenes be gloryus!

References

Hawks, K. (n.d.), *The joy of caning.* (retrieved: *https://www.geocities.ws/consvkink/ joy_of_caning_katharine_hawks*)

Hugs, L. (2004). *Caning and Rods—The Art of Caning.* (Found numerous places online, and text often varies from source to source. Having actually met Lady Hugs at a munch and chatted a bit, I can assure you she only wrote one version and that it has been perverted for unknown reasons as it has traveled around the internet.)

Bio

Dex

Dex is a covered Master who began his journey in the leather lifestyle over 26 years ago, embarking on an educational and self-reflective path of discovery. For several years, he led an extended leather family in upstate NY. His hospitality in his house of D/s, complete with dungeons in the attic and cellar, became legendary in the northeast.

He has since moved on but continues to hone his skills and grow as a Dominant. As a college professor (now retired), he loves teaching and sharing his knowledge. That, coupled with his love of learning in the lifestyle, naturally led to presenting. Dex taught his first lifestyle workshop within his first year in the D/s community.

Dex has since presented at numerous events and venues including: Anchor, T.I.E.D., Rose & Thorn, A.P.e.X., Albany Stocks & Bonds, A.K.P.C., Summer Bash, Spring Fling, Feel Me Breathe, The Floating World 2008, 2013 & 2014, Ohio SMART, Southeast Leatherfest 2009, 2010, 2011, 2023, & 2025, Kinko de Mayo 2011, SINSations in Leather 2010, Beyond Leather 2010, 2019, Thunder in the Mountains 2009, South Plains Leatherfest 2011, LeatherFET 2011,

Lupercalia MMXIV, Edmonton, Canada, Feel Me Breathe (FMB), Western Mass Power Exchange; E-P-I-C Lifestyle Conference 2016, Whips in Oakland Park, The Woodshed, Orlando, Tampa Phoenix Club, Sadovarius, Academy of Fetish Arts, Fetish Con 2017, The Society (Hartford, CT), Sin in the City 2019, TESfest 2019/2025, Weekend of Wickedness 2019/2022/2023/2024/2025, Jax FetFest 2019/2022/2024/2025, Savannah's Underground 2022/2025, the Vulgarians 2023/2024, Arizona Power Exchange 2024/2025, Leather Culture Club N.E. 2024, Carolina Coastal Fetish Fair 2024, and TESFest 2019/2025.

His first passion is the whip, but he does not confine himself to one love. His other interests include canes, the violet wand, bastinado, urethral sounds on females, and food play. He produces two lifestyle YouTube channels: The Leather Journey and Whips in the Dungeon. The instructional videos that complement his books: *Canes in the Dungeon, Whips in the Dungeon,* and *Variations and Vignettes* are hosted at http://witd.houseofgraves.com

www.ingramcontent.com/pod-product-compliance
Lightning Source LLC
Chambersburg PA
CBHW052051270326
41931CB00012B/2714